Money *Can* Buy Happiness

Money *Can* Buy Happiness

How to Spend to Get the Life You Want

MP Dunleavey

Broadway Books

New York

PUBLISHED BY BROADWAY BOOKS

Copyright © 2007 by MP Dunleavey

All Rights Reserved

Published in the United States by Broadway Books,
an imprint of The Doubleday Broadway Publishing Group,
a division of Random House, Inc., New York.
www.broadwaybooks.com

BROADWAY BOOKS and its logo, a letter B bisected on the diagonal,
are trademarks of Random House, Inc.

This title may be purchased for business or promotional use or for special sales. For information, please write to: Special Markets Department, Random House, Inc., 1745 Broadway, MD 6-3, New York, NY 10019, or specialmarkets@randomhouse.com.

BOOK DESIGN BY AMANDA DEWEY

Library of Congress Cataloging-in-Publication Data
Dunleavey, MP
   Money can buy happiness : how to spend to get the life you want /
MP Dunleavey. — 1st ed.
      p. cm.
   Includes bibliographical references and index.
   1. Finance, Personal.   2. Money.   3. Happiness.   I. Title.

HG179.D858 2007
333.024—dc22

2007000590

ISBN: 978-0-7679-2278-4

PRINTED IN THE UNITED STATES OF AMERICA

1   3   5   7   9   10   8   6   4   2

First Edition

For Matthew,
most beloved

Contents

Money *Can* Buy Happiness

Who Says Money Can't Buy Happiness?

While it's true that you can't go to Costco, plunk down your Visa, and get a lifetime supply of contentment—or good health, true love, or even a nice day—that doesn't mean the old cliché that "money can't buy happiness" is true. We're so obsessed with obtaining the material goods money can buy that we've lost track of the fact that happiness is one of the most powerful things money can buy. And that's what this book is about.

There are days when I just wish the salary fairy would wave her magic wand and quadruple my income. Or that the lottery fairy, her elusive twin sister, would slide a winning ticket under my pillow. *Then,* I sigh to myself, *then I'd be able to buy everything I want, and THEN I'd be happy!*

Unfortunately, the desire to have not just enough money but lots of money—stupid money, as they say—has evolved from a wistful fantasy to something of a cultural obsession. In just a couple of centuries we've gone from being a fledgling republic committed to "life, liberty, and the pursuit of happiness" to a nation of frenzied shoppers willing to commit bodily injury to take advantage of Wal-Mart's holiday sales.

Something is wrong.

People are working long hours, on top of even longer commutes, getting through one billing cycle so they can pay the next, leveraging their homes, spending so much on the present there's little saved for the future—all in the name of enjoying some mythic quality of life. So where is it?

THE AMERICAN DREAM?

Susan and Hazen, a couple I met in upstate New York, could write a modern parable about how the American Dream has gone awry.*

A few years ago these two really did have it all in the way that popular culture defines "having it all"—from their high-profile, jet-setting jobs to their spacious Brooklyn loft to trips abroad, nights at the theater, designer shopping sprees. But after they got married in 1997, they couldn't shake off a growing sense of dissatisfaction. "For my part, I got married because I wanted to spend time with Susan—and we weren't," says Hazen,

*Throughout this book, some names have been changed.

thirty-nine. "Either she was in London or I was in L.A., and even when we were both at home our schedules weren't jibing."

Susan, forty-three, had a similar epiphany. She'd achieved all the material goals she'd aimed for in her twenties—yet none of it was as satisfying as she'd dreamed. "You're on this path to consumerism, coming home with new clothes every weekend, or things for the house—all this stuff for very little gain in the end," she says. "We didn't get to spend more time doing the things we wanted to do—I didn't get to spend any more time painting or biking—because we were spending all this time working."

> **Certainly there are things in life that money can't buy, but it's very funny—did you ever try buying them without money?** —*Ogden Nash*

The irony of the fact that they were *each* earning six figures didn't escape either one of them. "You'd look at the numbers on the tax return and think: Where did it all go?" Hazen recalls.

Whether or not you bring home a six-figure income, I bet you've experienced some version of what Hazen and Susan were going through. When you've spent the better part of your adult life chasing a certain kind of "success" or "happiness," it's distressing to wake up to the fact that all you've earned isn't bringing you the wonderful life it was supposed to. Yet this has been the reality of consumer America for the last fifty years.

If I asked you whether America is, overall, a wealthier country now than it was after World War II, you'd probably say yes— and you'd be right. But if I asked whether our prosperity has made us happier as a people, you might hesitate. Despite living in possibly the richest country on earth, during the most prosperous time in history, researchers have found that Americans are not more satisfied with life, in general, than they were a few decades ago. According to a 2006 study by the Pew Research Center, between 1972 and 2004, Americans reported the same general level of happiness—despite the fact that during those decades the average per capita income more than doubled (accounting for inflation). "Thus, in the aggregate, Americans have more money now than they did a generation ago," the authors of the study wrote. "But in the aggregate, we're no happier."

In fact, when economists have studied the extraordinary growth in national and personal wealth in most Western countries in the last few decades, they've found that more cars, better appliances, and bigger homes—the most common measures of prosperity—have not boosted people's well-being one iota. Yet earning more, buying more, having more (and more) stuff seems to preoccupy us all, as though acquiring a certain lifestyle might bring the happiness we seek—as though we can afford to ignore the escalating level of financial insanity in our lives.

SPENDING IT ALL AND THEN SOME— FOR WHAT?

The total personal debt in this country, not including mortgages, is at an all-time high of more than $2.2 trillion—and climbing. People have become so accustomed to spending money they don't have that credit card debt has increased from $238 billion in 1989 to over $804 billion today. Bankruptcy rates have skyrocketed—with the highest number of filings among Americans aged 35 to 44, and the second-highest rates among young adults aged 25 to 34. And still we keep spending. In 1995, Americans borrowed about $11 billion in home equity— by 2005 that amount had soared to $243 billion. Granted, the real estate boom made it possible for countless homeowners to cash out money their homes had "earned," but to what end?

> **Annual income twenty pounds, annual expenditure nineteen six, result happiness. Annual income twenty pounds, annual expenditure twenty pound ought and six, result misery.** —*Charles Dickens*, David Copperfield

People now have so much stuff that the number of storage units nationwide increased from about 22,000 in the early nineties to nearly double that ten years later. That's *billions* of square feet designed to hold the things we've bought—and no longer use or need. The savings rate has plunged to its lowest level since the 1930s, dipping into negative numbers throughout much of 2005. While some economists quibble about those figures because they don't take into account certain types of savings, like home equity, the fact is that people are spending more—and saving less—of their disposable income than at any other time in history.

> **I had more clothes than I had closets, more cars than garage space, but no money.** —*Sammy Davis Jr.*

Yet this nonstop elbowing for material success means that instead of becoming enriched, we are depleted. In getting and spending we lose our irreplaceable time, our valuable energy, our personal and spiritual creativity. Worse, we are slowly forgetting how to invest our money in ways that do make us happy.

First and foremost, I'd like you to see this as an investment book. Instead of focusing on bonds and mutual funds, I'm going to show you how to invest your time, energy, and above all your money in your own long-term, tax-free, high-yield happiness. Which is exactly what Hazen and Susan finally decided to do a couple of years ago.

The turning point came when they began to look at their quality of life the same way an investor weighs the performance of stocks in his portfolio. If spending all their time and energy and money in pursuit of success wasn't giving them the quality of life they dreamed of, what would? They knew what their priorities were: "We knew we both loved the outdoors, we loved to travel—and we loved to work," says Hazen. They also knew they didn't want to live in an urban area anymore, and they wanted to spend more time together. The time had come to invest their resources in the life they wanted. But how?

First they bought a weekend house, which gave them a taste of the more rural lifestyle they wanted. The next hurdle was finding a way to earn a living outside the urban corporate jungle. So the two began to investigate ways that they could run a business in the countryside that would generate a steady income. It took them over a year of research and wrangling with each other before they arrived at the idea of starting an alpaca farm, which they combined with a marketing company that would cater to other alpaca breeders—a decision that gave them the income they needed, plus the quality of life they wanted, and then some (you can check out their business at www.hasu.biz).

And when they look back at the hectic, acquisitive life they used to lead, they both shudder. "Wow," says Hazen. "I would never go back to that."

IT'S NOT IF YOU SPEND, BUT HOW

Before we continue, I want to address any fears you might have that this book will drag you down the well-worn path to Walden Pond, and demand that you renounce all your worldly possessions and live off the land. I'm not going to tell you to take a vow of poverty, build a log cabin, grow your own broccoli, and give more to Greenpeace—or raise alpacas. Starting an alpaca farm isn't my idea of the good life, and it may not be yours, and that's fine. The point is that Susan and Hazen were able to reinvest their assets in a way of life that was fulfilling to them.

That's what you'll be doing as you move through this book.

While I'm all in favor of giving more to environmental causes and retreating to your own personal Walden (if that's what does it for you), I would never insist that anyone reject all the lovely, concrete, fun stuff that adds to the enjoyment of life. It's just that when you focus only on the *things* money can buy, you lose out on a bigger, broader, more satisfying life.

This isn't exactly news. For millennia, spiritual leaders from every corner of the globe have made the same point: The pursuit of money and material things alone leads to a persistent sense of emptiness. Today a spate of studies from the fields of economics and psychology add scientific support for that age-old notion. Yet that hollow feeling is what many people face every single day. Many of us sense that we're at the mercy of drives that don't enrich our lives, but it's hard to break free of the siren song of materialism: *Earn more, buy more, and ye shall be happy this time, really.* That's not to say that all material pleasures will lure you onto the rocks of misery and self-destruction, but what a bumper crop of research seems to show—and what many of us sense instinctively—is that buying into and onto the endless treadmill of today's consumer culture is guaranteed to keep you out of sync with the stuff that leads to a truly happier life.

It's not that money makes no difference: When an income boost can pull people up and out of poverty, their sense of well-being increases. But studies show that once the basics of life are taken care of—having a place to live, enough to eat, access to health care—more income doesn't necessarily increase quality of life significantly. One eye-opening study found that when people in different countries, at a range of income levels, were asked to rate their quality of life—those living in what many would consider poverty in Calcutta rated their overall contentment a 4.6, on a scale of 1 to 10. By comparison, Americans rated their well-being a 5.8—just a little higher, despite being vastly more wealthy, at least in material terms.

Why would people living in an impoverished developing nation declare themselves nearly as content as citizens of a supposedly far richer country? Because what studies by psychologists, sociologists, and economists have demonstrated over and over again is that true and lasting happiness doesn't revolve around what you earn and own, but on a more human sort of capital: your connections to others, time to enjoy living, your health, satisfying pursuits, and for many people a spiritual life.

THE "STUFF" OF HAPPINESS

A few years ago, Princeton economist and Nobel Prize winner Daniel Kahneman did an experiment in which he asked some nine hundred working women to divide up a single day into segments, note which activities they spent their time on during each segment, and which they enjoyed most. In order of preference, the top six things that made them happiest were:

Sex
Socializing
Relaxing
Praying/worshipping/meditating
Eating
Exercising

This study attracted a lot of attention for a couple of reasons. First, I think people are always curious to know what makes for happiness, their own or anyone else's. Second, the answers struck a lot of people as being exceptionally ordinary. You don't see "driving my Lexus" or "sunning in St. Tropez" at the top of this list. The activities these women found most rewarding revolved around being connected to others, to themselves, to the contemplative aspect of their lives, and to their own physical well-being. (And to food—not a bad source of pleasure.)

Granted, this was in some ways a simple study. Kahneman asked these women to reflect on the previous day, note the people they were with, the various activities they'd been engaged in, and how they felt while they were doing them. They could have said anything. And yet to an astonishing degree their responses confirm what countless other studies about happiness seem to show: There are certain core elements in life that we humans seem to find immensely satisfying, no matter who we are or where we live or what sort of background we hail from.

Some 2,500 years ago, Aristotle wrote extensively about what comprised "the good life." He believed that a satisfying life consisted of many parts: "[G]ood birth, plenty of friends, good friends, wealth, good children, plenty of children, a happy old age, and also such bodily excellences as health, beauty, strength, large stature, athletic powers, together with fame, honor, good luck, and excellence." While certain things differ from the modern-day list above, you can see that even a couple of thousand years ago, what defined quality of life wasn't so different. And guess what? Researchers have yet to find that making a million bucks or going on a grand shopping spree is part of that package.

What is part of that package? In the coming chapters I'll examine why so many of us have become overinvested in acquiring stuff that's not so fulfilling—and explain how to invest your money, time, and other resources into a set of core assets that will yield a much bigger gain in terms of your deepest well-being.

While there's plenty of individual variation in what makes for a rewarding life, some of the fundamental elements include:

- Being involved with family, friends, and community
- Having more time for yourself
- Developing your skills, passions, and strengths
- Easing financial stress
- Enhancing your health on all levels
- Having more fun (a lot more, I hope)
- Securing your financial future
- Finding meaningful, enjoyable ways to give to others

> **I don't continually question my reason to live. It's just a state of being. The real question is what you're doing with the living you're doing, and what you want to be doing with that living.** —*Mick Jagger*

There's absolutely nothing surprising on this list, nothing new—except the radical idea that these aren't philosophical choices, but financial ones. For that reason, I've devoted certain sections of the book to helping you strengthen your basic personal finance skills. If I've learned one thing during the years I've been writing about money—specifically about people's financial quirks, faux pas, failings, and blind spots—it's that creating financial sanity is the bedrock of living a happy life. So although a large part of this book is about understanding what makes for happiness, the rest is about cultivating the financial habits that will support these changes. First, I'll address where your money goes and why, and then we'll tackle tougher topics like how to get out of debt and save for a secure future—all of which are essential to your ultimate happiness.

As you gradually invest your resources in a more rewarding way of life, it will become clear that when used wisely—you bet money can buy happiness. The next chapter is about building a portfolio of investments, so to say, that will yield a happier life.

1

Your Happiness
Portfolio

There is a gigantic difference between earning
a great deal of money and being rich.

—Marlene Dietrich

For centuries, economists based their theories on the premise that man was a "rational actor" who could be counted on to make economic decisions in his own best interests at all times. (I know, I laughed when I learned that, too.)

As anyone who has put an overpriced vacation on Visa—or spent part of their rent money on clothes—can attest, neither man nor woman is terribly rational when it comes to making economic decisions. You know what you want—yet you go ahead and spend your money on something else. Just look at all the data on retirement: Repeated surveys have found that people aren't saving enough for retirement; moreover, people *know* that they aren't saving enough for retirement. Yet what are people most worried about? Not having enough money in retirement!

These inconsistencies don't affect just how well we plan ahead; they seem to be a flaw in the way human beings were designed to think and act financially. That's why it's important to be aware of your own mixed impulses as you think about using your money to make you happier. Let's do a short, fun exercise so you can see what I mean regarding some of your own quality-of-life choices thus far.

EXERCISE

The Cost of Living

This exercise works like the old "Mad Libs," but it's a little more free-form. Just fill in the blanks with adjectives, verbs, nouns, whatever. Add words where you need to, improvise if you feel like it—have fun, be honest, and see what emerges. Time required: About two minutes, if that.

1. I earn a living by _____; I consider my job to be _____.

2. My dream job or career would be _____.

3. My home is _____ and a realtor would describe the location as _____ and _____.

4. After work I usually _____ and _____.

5. On the weekend I typically _____ and _____.

6. The top three things I spend money on are
_____ , _____ ,
and _____.

7. I'd describe my friends as _____ ;
when we see each other we usually _____
_____.

8. My family is _____ and I sometimes
wish I could _____.

9. The main things that keep me up at night are
_____.

10. The three areas where my time is most committed are
_____ , _____ , and _____.

11. My spiritual life consists of _____ and I feel
_____ about that.

12. Sometimes I feel like my life is missing _____
_____.

13. When I have a free hour or two, I usually _____
_____ or _____.

14. My last vacation was _____ and it was
_____.

15. If I could change three things about my life, they would
be _____ , _____ , and _____.

16. When I'm eighty, I hope to look back on a life that was
_____ , _____ , and _____.

Ideally, this exercise should make you feel somewhat surprised or even uncomfortable. Or it might provoke a moment of clarity. When my husband did a test run of this exercise for me, he put down his pen and said, "Well, I've just figured out that I hate my job." He knew that already, but these questions do have a way of giving you a fly-on-the-wall perspective so you can see how various lifestyle choices interconnect—and whether those choices are in sync with what's most important or valuable to you.

> **What's money? A man is a success if he gets up in the morning and goes to bed at night and in between does what he wants to do.**   —*Bob Dylan*

Now, as you begin to think like a happiness investor, here are some questions to ask yourself (you don't have to write anything down here, but do take a couple of minutes to consider your answers):

- What surprised you about some of the answers you gave?
- Did you notice any discrepancies between where your resources go and what you find most satisfying in life?
- What are some ways that you're using your money, time, or energy that yield the biggest payoff in terms of your own happiness?
- What are some of the ways you're using your money, time, or energy for paltry gains?
- If you could change one thing this week, maybe even today, that might be a better investment in your own happiness, what would it be?

LIFE IS RICH: INVEST WISELY

It may seem strange to equate your personal well-being with an investment portfolio, but it's a pretty useful metaphor. It reminds you, the stockholder, that you have a fair amount of control over where you invest and why. And just as every financial investor has very different stakes in his or her portfolio, it's the same with happiness. Savvy money managers may know to put a certain amount of capital into something solid like bonds, blue chip stocks, or large-cap mutual funds, but the precise investments they choose are up to each individual. Likewise, how you decide to balance your assets in order to enhance your own happiness is ultimately up to you.

After all, how people define happiness is an extremely subjective matter, not to say downright idiosyncratic at times. It's pretty amazing to imagine the myriad types of joy, pleasure, contentment, and elation each person can have—even within a single day:

- There's the deliciousness of your first sip of coffee in the morning . . .
- the thrill of overcoming a challenge . . .
- the bliss of lying in the sun . . .
- the physical rush of exercise . . .
- the peace you feel while watching a child sleep . . .
- the fun of fall-off-your-chair laughter with friends . . .
- the satisfaction of doing your best . . .
- the joy when you hold someone you love . . .

- the tingly relief of a shower after a sweaty workout . . .
- the excitement when you've landed a new job . . .
- the ordinary happiness of knowing, thank God, it's Friday.

You could add dozens of items to this list, and so could I, but the bigger question is: How do you decide which type of happiness to invest in? Are some investments better than others?

Yes, as it turns out, some are. Eons of human experience plus quite a bit of research have left a fairly thick trail of bread crumbs that show where the path to happiness lies. And as your official happiness adviser, those are the stocks that I'm going to recommend you put at the heart of your portfolio. I've outlined them below and will explore them in detail in the coming chapters.

ASSET #1: YOUR VALUABLE TIME

People talk about how much time they spend doing this or that, but how often do you think about the "spending" part of the equation? Yet how you spend or save or waste your time has just as much of an impact on your quality of life as the way you choose to spend your cash. Chapter 3 is about the trade-offs you can make to reclaim your time—and invest in a happier life.

ASSET #2: YOUR PERSONAL RESOURCES

When talking about happiness, Aristotle used the Greek word *eudaimonia*—which doesn't refer to the upbeat outlook we moderns associate with being happy, but rather to the life well-lived: the inner satisfaction you gain when you live up to your strengths and make the most of your talents. Today the field of positive psychology has generated numerous studies about the immense benefit of being engaged in activities that stretch the envelope of who you are—and that by being more active and positive in your approach to your own life and goals, it is possible to up your happiness quotient. Investing in yourself is what chapter 4 is all about.

ASSET #3: YOUR HEALTH

Most people think of good health as a positive thing on its own. Investing in your health as a means of increasing your total well-being is still a relatively new idea, even though science supports the rather obvious conclusion that healthier people are happier. Chapter 6 shows how small but steady investments in your physical plant are key to the overall performance of your portfolio. (Besides, shoring up your physical well-being will save you money in the long run—dividends that you can use to further invest in your quality of life as well.)

ASSET #4: FINANCIAL CONTROL

For many people, worrying about money has become a way of life—and scientists are now connecting persistent financial angst with serious mental and physical ailments. Small wonder that learning better money management skills in order to invest in your own ongoing financial sanity is so important. In chapters 3, 7, 8, and 9, I'll show you how to ditch bad money habits, vanquish debt, buy yourself greater peace of mind—and take control of your future. If you feel euphoric at the very thought of a stress-free, well-ordered financial life—you know what a vital part of your happiness portfolio this will be.

ASSET #5: MUTUAL FUN

You don't need me to sell you on the importance of developing a strong fun strategy. (And you don't need to see *The Shining* to know that "all work and no play" really doesn't work out well for anyone in the end.) In chapter 10 we'll tackle the all-important fun sector and the countless ways it can boost your portfolio's overall performance. I'll also reveal the groundbreaking results of my Highly Unscientific National Fun Survey.

ASSET #6: GET INTO BONDS

Scientists squabble about whether happier people tend to have more active social lives—or whether having vibrant connections to others makes you happier. It's possible to see the issue either way, but one thing seems indisputable: We are people who need people, as the schmaltzy old song goes. The correlation between having friends, being part of a community and/or close to your family, and being happy is a strong one. The data on the long-term benefits of marriage are also striking.

That doesn't mean you have to win a popularity contest or leap into a romantic relationship to be happier. But investing more in the people who are most important to you is essential to having a life that's fulfilling. More on that in chapter 11.

ASSET #7: GIVING TO FEEL GOOD

Donating your time and money to help others is always presented as the "right" thing to do. The fact that it makes you feel good, too, has been largely ignored as a minor fringe benefit. Now researchers are finding that the act of giving bestows numerous gifts on the giver as well: It supports and strengthens social bonds, enriches your life, enhances your health, and even boosts longevity. It's like discovering that eating a can of spinach really will turn you into a hero, although I promise chapter 12 makes no mention of eating your vegetables.

INVESTOR'S CHOICE

So does this mean you must invest in this little lineup of so-called happiness stocks or risk a life of low returns? Nope. These are just some of the areas that researchers have found that contribute to personal satisfaction and quality of life. Only you can decide how you want to invest this portfolio of yours. In the financial world, people use different methods to determine their asset allocation—and the same seems to be true of well-being: How you choose to allocate *your* assets will be based on numerous factors in your own life.

In early 2006, I attended a symposium on Economics and Happiness at the University of Southern California. There I met Mariano Rojas, an economist at the Universidad de las Americas in Puebla, Mexico, whose research supports the idea that happiness is a mix, you might say, of different stocks.

Rojas surveyed 579 people in five districts in Mexico about their overall well-being, and then asked how satisfied they were in various areas of life—work and career, family and community, health, and so on. Like many economists, he found that some arenas have a greater impact on people's contentment with life—for example, a rewarding family life was a key ingredient in overall life satisfaction, whereas work tended not to have as big an impact. But Rojas also found that it's possible to increase your individual happiness by investing more in the areas that will have the most impact for you—and less in those that don't. "Hence a person who is very unsatisfied in her family domain and satisfied in her economic domains may benefit the most from an increase in family rather than [increasing] economic satisfaction," Rojas writes.

His point isn't that we all need to invest in the same things, but rather that the way people choose to invest in their happiness is "contingent on a person's own circumstances." If you're in good health and have a happy home life, you don't need to invest more in those domains. Rather, like any savvy investor, you're better off paying more attention to the sectors of your portfolio that aren't delivering the returns you'd like to see. Perhaps you need to have more fun, to reduce stress, spend more time with friends, or find more time for yourself.

The essential thing to remember as you go through this book is that "joy" and "satisfaction" and "happiness" aren't just pleasant, abstract notions; investing in a happier way of life requires making new decisions about how you spend your money and time.

DO YOU *REALLY* KNOW WHAT'S BEST FOR YOU?

For years, Wendy and Peter didn't think they could afford anything but the lifestyle they had. They were both working full-time jobs in a big West Coast city. Peter commuted an hour to and from work. They earned quite a good living, but that was paling beside the escalating levels of stress in their lives. "We were emotionally, mentally, and physically depleted—and I had all kinds of health issues that were made worse by the way we were living," Wendy says. "Peter was exhausted by driving an hour each way. He would come home at 7:30, our daughter went to bed at 8:00, and that was his day."

Like many people, for years the two struggled to figure a way out of all these demands. Maybe Wendy could quit her job or work part-time; maybe they could live on less. But as we all know, it's hard to make a change when the treadmill of life just keeps moving forward, pulling you with it. Then, Peter was offered a job in another city—and that became the catalyst they both needed to invest in a new way of life.

Peter now had a ten-minute commute to his job. Wendy wasn't sure what would happen when she left her job—but it turned out that her managers were willing to make it work long-distance. So what she feared might be a flying leap into unemployment turned out to be a gentle step into telecommuting—but at a reduced salary. "I started working twenty-four hours a week and took a huge pay cut," she says, "but it's been worth every penny."

Did she and her husband have to cut back, watch what they spent, become more careful with money? Sure, but not nearly as much as they'd feared. Even though they now were making less, it turned out that with more time to devote to their newly sane life, the two were better money managers. "We didn't have the energy before," Wendy admits.

Besides, for the income they gave up, what they've gained by making their time a priority investment is priceless, Wendy says. "I don't feel sick when I wake up in the morning. In the old mode I could never get caught up. Our marriage has improved because we're not so stressed that we bark at each other all the time."

And of course Wendy gets to spend much more time with her rapidly growing daughter, walking her to school, going to the zoo, but most of all just . . . being there. "Last summer I was right there when she was playing with her friends in the sprinkler on the front lawn. And I just thought: This is fabulous—this is worth half my salary, to be here with all these goofy kids throwing water balloons."

ARE YOU HAPPIER ON PAPER?

Like Peter and Wendy, most of us get so preoccupied with getting by that the idea of consciously investing money in a happier way of life gets lost in the sauce of paying bills and putting dinner on the table and fixing the car and trying to have a good time every once in a while. It's hard to imagine making significantly different financial choices when most of us can barely afford our current way of life. Live happier—what's that going to cost? Here's another exercise that will provide a fresh perspective on the financial side of your quality-of-life decisions.

EXERCISE

It's 10 P.M., Do You Know Where Your Money Is?

What you'll need: A piece of paper and a pen or pencil. Time required: about six minutes.

1. 1 Minute: Make a list of things that make you happy. I know, it's a little like "These are a few of my favorite things . . . ," but don't take it too seriously. This should be fun. Sunsets, egg creams, traveling, talking to your best friend, watching your kids play soccer, winning that eBay auction—just take one minute to scribble down whatever happinesses, small and large, present and past, come to mind.

2. 2 Minutes: Without thinking too hard, write down whatever you can remember about how you spent your money in the last couple of weeks. You don't have to recall every last cup of coffee or tank of gas. If you paid the phone bill, but you can't remember how much it was, ballpark it. If you went out to dinner with friends, or bought a new suit or a gift, jot down your best guesstimate. Hint: If you're looking for receipts in your wallet, you're taking this too seriously. Just write down whatever you can for now.

3. Now, reread the happiness list and put a dollar sign next to the things that cost money.

4. Next, read over list #2 and note whether any of your expenditures also made you happy, for example, going to the movies. (Even if you think you can smell where this is going, it's illuminating to complete the whole thing.)

5. In the graph below you'll see two bars. Let each one represent your net income for the past month, whatever that amount is. Next to the bar on the left, draw another bar that represents the rough portion of your monthly income that went toward the expenses from list #2.

6. Next to the income bar on the right, draw a bar that represents the portion of your income this past month that went toward things that make you happy.

Although this exercise doesn't examine how you spend each dime—we'll do a more thorough spending overview later—it provides a snapshot of your asset allocation strategy, if you will, thus far. Money can buy happiness, yes, but only when you start to reevaluate where you're putting your financial resources—and why.

Here are some questions to ask about your financial habits and assumptions:

- Most people believe they spend their money primarily on life's essentials, or on things that are important to them. What do you see when you look at your list of expenses?
- People often tell themselves that they would like to spend more money on enjoying life, but they can't afford to. When you look at the list of stuff that makes you happy, do you think that's true, or could you envision investing more money in those activities?
- Do you notice any overlap between your happiness list and the assets outlined above that I recommend putting at the heart of your personal portfolio?
- Financial advisers often use pie charts to show the breakdown of assets in a portfolio. Below is a sample pie chart that shows how someone might invest their money in different assets. Try making your own "happiness allocation" pie chart. You can use the assets listed above, plus your own. Note the areas where you'd like to invest more than you are currently.

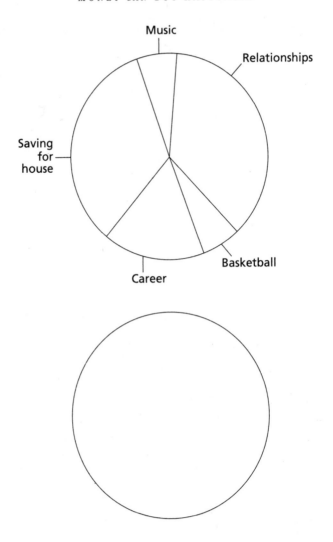

Now we're getting to the financial side of the equation. In the next chapter we'll talk more about the powerful factors that misguide our financial lives, and look at simple ways to start putting more of your money where your happiness lies.

2

Buy Yourself
Less Stuff

The world is too much with us; late and soon,
Getting and spending, we lay waste our powers.

—*William Wordsworth*

As I mentioned in the last chapter, we humans seem to suffer from a fundamental flaw when it comes to making a connection between money and happiness. The problem doesn't arise so much with the things we buy, but with our expectations for the extent to which material goods can really improve our quality of life.

Many years ago, Steve, now sixty, was a lieutenant in the army, stationed on the West Coast with his wife and baby daughter. Life was good, but he knew one thing would make it perfect: a Jaguar XKE—"the most beautiful production car ever made," he says. "I always thought, 'If only I could have an XKE, it would make me so happy!' So finally I said, damn, I'm going to buy me a Jaguar."

He couldn't afford to buy a new one, so he set his sights on finding the most perfect "pre-owned" XKE that he could. Steve remembers poring over the classified ads until he found the right one, and he paid about $2,500 for it—a huge sum in those days. At first it was everything he'd dreamed of: sleek, classy, and luxurious. He really couldn't have been a happier guy. Wife, daughter, Jaguar XKE—what more does a man need from life? But soon the joy began to ebb. In fact, he says, "That car made me miserable. It was temperamental and high-maintenance, and as soon as you'd fix one thing another thing would break."

The constant maintenance wore on his nerves and strained his marriage. (One low point, he says, was when his wife found him obsessively scrubbing the hubcaps in the bathtub.) But it wasn't the upkeep that was such a letdown, but that such a major purchase could be so disappointing. It was a huge financial investment that didn't yield the kind of ongoing golden glow of satisfaction he'd assumed it would. Finally, he sold the Jaguar and faced a lesson he never forgot. "It taught me that things *really* don't make you happy," Steve says.

I doubt you're surprised by Steve's revelation; most people could have told him before he bought the car that it would brighten his life by only so much. Yet no matter how often we remind ourselves—"Hey, that new car/stereo/granite countertop is going to make me only so happy"—it doesn't seem to diminish the constant craving so many of us have for bigger, better, shinier, faster, more high-tech stuff. Or the fantasy that somewhere up the chain of purchases, you'll hit the one that finally completes you.

Perhaps you're one of those enlightened souls who has already put materialism in perspective. If so, I salute you—but as a fellow consumer, I'm also a little skeptical. Here's why.

Nearly forty years ago, Richard Easterlin, now an economist at the University of Southern California, began examining people's material desires and how they felt once they achieved those goals. Easterlin reviewed surveys of thousands of Americans, who said they believed the good life consisted of owning certain things—like having a nice car, pool, vacation home, and so on. While they themselves had only 1.7 of the desired items, they felt that owning 4.4 (on average) would constitute a satisfactory life.

That seems reasonable. You don't quite have all the things you want, but you're sure that when you acquire them, you'll be satisfied.

But when Easterlin then studied people's responses to the same questions many years later, he found that although on average people now owned 3.1 of the desired goods—now they believed they wouldn't achieve the so-called good life until they owned 5.6 of them.

You can see how the underlying itch to acquire more (and more) turns into a never-ending treadmill of consumption—not because the things we want are bad, but because we attach to them an impossible outcome: that certain possessions can and will increase our happiness.

The confounding factor is that owning and buying stuff actually *is* fun. It's a normal, natural part of life—one of the perks of having to spend your allotted time on planet earth. But a problem unfolds when the momentary kick fades, and your natural instinct is to want to achieve that feel-good state again somehow.

So you strive for the next thing, in the belief that maybe if you get more bang for your buck, this time it will last.

> **After a time, you may find that having is not so pleasing a thing, after all, as wanting. It is not logical, but it is often true.** —*Mr. Spock*

Unfortunately, a buck can buy only so much bang, and very quickly you're caught on what researchers have dubbed the "hedonic treadmill," the ceaseless quest for *moremoremore* that drives our lives, dominates our thoughts, and erodes our quality of life.

THE GRASS *IS* ALWAYS GREENER

Why? Because people have an astonishing ability to adapt to almost any circumstance, positive or negative, with little change in our overall sense of well-being. Even studies of cancer patients and paraplegics have shown that people whom most of us would imagine to be depressed or suffering actually report being about as happy as healthy folks—because they've adapted to their lives. To be sure, a calamity like a sudden death, divorce, or job loss can be traumatic and isn't something you adjust to quickly at all. But the bulk of human experiences, *especially when it comes to most monetary or material gains,* have a surprisingly short-lived effect on how happy you are.

Alas, that's not what most of us believe. You may have felt the whirring of that treadmill underfoot after a Saturday shopping at the mall, or when you finished renovating the kitchen or splurged on a hand-tailored suit or an expensive new watch. It's not that those things didn't bring you pleasure. You were probably thrilled at first. It's just that within a fairly short time the excitement fades. Life returns to normal. You still squabble with your mate. Your boss is a pain. You haven't lost that five pounds. So you start looking for the next big thrill—and back on the treadmill you go.

I remember when I was earning $18,000 a year, in my first job after college. If only I could make $35,000, I recall telling a friend, I would be totally happy—I'd have everything I needed.

A few years later, when I was making $35,000 a year, I realized all I needed was an income of $50,000. That seemed reasonable. Life was so hard on a mere $35,000. Get me $15,000 more and my problems would vanish!

Then, when I was making $50,000 (this all really happened), it was clear to me: I needed to make at least $80,000 to be okay, but $100,000—that magic six-figure number—was what it would take to *truly* give me the life I wanted, shore up my insecurities, and finally vanquish any and all lingering problems.

The never-ending upward spiral seems clear now, and yet it took me years to see that I was caught in the Must Have More cycle that defines modern life.

THE UNDERLYING POWER OF MONEY

So how do you get off the hamster wheel of "getting and spending" in order to invest in a happier way of life? These choices don't happen overnight. You can't call your happiness broker at Merrill Lynch and say, "Get me some shares of happiness, and sell this treadmill stuff, will ya? It's going nowhere." If only it were that simple.

In order to shift your focus away from stuff in order to invest more in life, it helps to understand some of the powerful dynamics, both internal and external, that may be influencing how and why you invest your financial resources.

Money and the Brain

Some scientists have speculated that the acquisition of money and things creates a kind of dopamine rush in the brain, similar to addiction, which may be one reason why it's hard for people to stop chasing after material thrills. Others have pointed out that human beings are hardwired, from an evolutionary perspective, to compete for the best and most of any goods available. This "keeping up with the Joneses" that we all know and dread thus contributes to what Harvard psychologist Daniel Gilbert has called "the cycle of miswanting," because people feel compelled to invest in the things that won't make them happy instead of the things that do.

Money and Competition

Most people are striving to find that balance, but as we all know it's a constant struggle—and it's not new. With the publication of *The Theory of the Leisure Class* in 1899, economist Thorstein Veblen coined the term "conspicuous consumption" to describe a phenomenon that will sound as contemporary as *InStyle* magazine. Conspicuous consumption is not about buying things you need, but about buying things as a symbol of your earning power, a signal to others that you've attained a certain level of wealth. These days conspicuous consumption has escalated into an even more aggressive form of one-upmanship that some call "competitive consumption." That's the desire to have things that not only display your purchasing power, but your ability to outstrip whatever your neighbor just acquired.

Materialism and Your Neighbor

As I mentioned in the last chapter, we are all vulnerable to the financial and material influences of the environment in which we live—never mind the pervasive power of media and advertising. But as much as you want to believe you're in charge of your own behavior, it pays to be aware of the impact that others' behavior may have on your own "investment" decisions, whether you know it or not.

> **Never keep up with the Joneses. Drag them down to your level. It's cheaper.** —*Quentin Crisp*

This was captured in an article I read about the phenomenon of automaticity—the fascinating and depressing human tendency to imitate what's going on around us. One study found that when people were told to complete a task next to an experimenter who, for example, often rubbed her face, subjects likewise tended to rub their faces, even though afterward they had no idea that the experimenter's fidgeting had been "contagious." Another study found that when people were merely shown a series of words associated with being elderly, they behaved in a more elderly manner (i.e., walked slower, were more forgetful)—again, without realizing they had succumbed to a series of covert directions, if you will.

It's not hard to imagine, then, the impact on your own financial desires when a friend spends twenty minutes relating her latest shopping extravaganza, describing her new Bose stereo, or has you take a spin in her cute new customized, fully loaded Mini Cooper.

INFLATION OF OUR EXPECTATIONS

So although it may seem obvious that buying less stuff will provide you with extra resources to invest in a happier way of life, every day you have to fend off a series of stealth assaults on your financial sanity—including the steady inflation of your own expectations for what a so-called "normal" or "average" life consists of.

Witness the average size of a new single-family home. In the early 1970s it was 1,500 square feet. As of early 2005 the average home size had grown to 2,400 square feet—and with it, people's expectations of how big an "average" home should be as well as which amenities should come with it, says Gopal Ahluwalia, vice president of research for the National Association of Home Builders.

What was once considered upscale is now the "new normal" for homeowners today, Ahluwalia says: from his and hers walk-in closets in the master bedroom to kitchen islands with cooktops to three-car garages. (People don't want a three-car garage because they have three cars, he added, but because they want to make sure they have enough storage for all their excess stuff.)

Nor have home sizes increased because people have bigger families. In the last thirty-five years, Ahluwalia says, the average family size declined to 2.11 people from 3.58.

That hasn't stopped people from spending a lot more money for an expanded way of life—whether or not they can afford it. No wonder Americans are experiencing an epidemic of debt and bankruptcy, the likes of which has never been seen before.

IF ONLY BIGGER WAS ALWAYS BETTER

How do you combat the multitude of forces that influence how you spend your money and live your life? The first step is to become better acquainted with the joys of "inconspicuous consumption."

Inconspicuous consumption doesn't get a lot of airtime; you can't get it on sale at Kmart; Wal-Mart doesn't carry big tubs of it at a discount. The less-tangible pleasures in life rarely have the same wow power as things, even though they are more deeply satisfying. The core assets in the happiness portfolio I outlined in the last chapter are all based on inconspicuous consumption—spending less on stuff and more on life.

EXERCISE

Your Money and/or Your Life

To illustrate the contrast between conspicuous material desires and inconspicuous ones, Cornell economist Robert Frank created a series of thought experiments (below). The questions are based on his model, which you can find in his excellent book about the escalating insanity of materialism, *Luxury Fever.* There are no right answers—just read each one and think about it.

1. If you could live in a 4,000-square-foot home and have one week of vacation a year, or live in a 2,000-square-foot home and have three weeks' vacation, which would you choose?

2. If you could have a job that paid $200,000 a year, but you could only see your friends once a month, vs. a job that paid $100,000 and you could see your friends every week—which would you choose?

3. If you could buy a new 3,000-square-foot house for $400,000 (incurring a hefty mortgage) or an older home of the same size that would require some work for $200,000 (and more affordable monthly payments), which would you choose?

4. If you could land a job at the top of your profession, but you got to see your children for only a handful of hours a week, vs. keeping a job with less prestige, but which gave you a flexible schedule—which would you choose?

I love these brain twisters because they're a potent reminder that many of the assumptions we all live with—that the bigger house or better job is always the more desirable choice—may not be deep down what we want at all. In fact, it would be wise to consider whether choosing the alternatives might be the high road to a much more satisfying quality of life.

A few years ago Kurt and Diane, a couple in their thirties, seemed like poster children for conspicuous consumption—from their four-bedroom house in a nice suburb of Chicago to their shiny Subaru.

But they weren't happy. They both missed living in the city, where they'd gone to college (and where many of their friends still lived). They found caring for their big house and yard a drag; Kurt hated his long commute. So they did the opposite of what many people aspire to: They sold their house, sold their car, and moved back to the city. "We never felt comfortable living in that house," Diane admits. "It wasn't the life we wanted at all. It was too isolated. And what did we need all that space for?" Come to find out, spending their money on a less conspicuous home in a more culture-rich, friend-centric city held the most meaning for them.

Kurt and Diane didn't end up living frugally on a farm somewhere—they would have been miserable. In fact, they didn't end up spending any less money. But they did decide to invest their money in less conspicuous ways that would make them conspicuously happier.

Instead of an hour-long commute to and from work, it now takes Kurt fifteen minutes to get to the office, so he has more time to focus on his side business in graphic design and hang out with the family. Their son's preschool is within walking distance of their home, so they can take turns walking him to school. If they need a car, they rent one. The couple has easy access to restaurants, museums, countless cultural events, and they can see their friends more often.

That's inconspicuous consumption—and for the most part that's what your happiness portfolio is based on. The key financial principle here is buying less stuff so you can invest in the more durable pleasures of life. But in order to do so, you need to put your personal finance cap on, because the next step requires you to start taking the reins of your financial life by learning where your money goes—and then deciding if that's where you really want it to go.

FOLLOW THE MONEY: YOU'LL BE GLAD YOU DID

In my experience, many people—even some quite successful people—have only a vague idea about where their money goes on a daily, monthly, or yearly basis. And most people hate keeping a so-called spending diary to monitor their expenditures, in part because it's tedious, but mainly because they're afraid of what they'll find.

But the reality is that if you want to upgrade your quality of life, you're going to need to take control over your money to do it—so some sort of overview is needed. So let's make it simple: Rather than asking you to keep a diary of what you spend, I'd like you to keep a record of whether what you spend is being invested in the pursuit of happiness.

In many ways using financial software is the fastest way to track where your money goes. I've used software and found it extremely useful—and these days programs like Excel, Quicken, and Money are easier to use than ever.

> **Money is like an arm or a leg—use it or lose it.**
>
> —*Henry Ford, interview with the* New York Times,
> *November 8, 1931*

If you have the patience, another money-tracking method is to read through your credit card and bank statements, reviewing every bill paid, every credit and debit purchase (although this won't tell you where that hundred-dollar ATM cash withdrawal went).

For me, nothing beats carrying around an envelope in your purse, briefcase, or backpack into which you put every single last receipt you get, every day, for a month. Keep a pen handy so you can jot down random items for which you don't have a receipt, like bills you pay or your monthly commuting pass or the seventy-five cents you put in a parking meter.

You also can do some combination of the above: Use software (Money, Excel, Quicken) for all bank transactions; use the envelope to track cash; double-check your statements. Or if little pieces of paper drive you nuts, just keep a detailed spending notebook and forget the receipts. The point is, do whatever works for you, but find a way to monitor how and why and where your money goes for at least two weeks.

Three points:

1. You're not doing this to feel guilty about how much you spend on cigarettes or DVDs or the fact that you got another late charge on your credit card. You're doing this because you want to take control over your money in order to enjoy your life to the hilt.

2. Do this exercise with a friend, otherwise you are likely to crap out—as is only human.

3. Expect yourself to have trouble at first. As with taking up exercise or quitting smoking, you may need a few tries. Don't sweat it. Few people like to do this and even fewer stick to it. Just try. Take a break if you get sick of it. Then try again next week. It's a good idea to attempt this exercise a couple of times a year anyway while you're reorganizing your financial closets. It keeps you focused on your greater goals.

Now, make a list of recent expenses on the worksheet here, and note whether each one has increased your happiness dividends—and if so, in what way. Here is a sample:

Expense	Cost	Happiness Portfolio?	How?
cell phone	$75	Yes ☐ No ☑	
mortgage	$1,179	Yes ☑ No ☐	security; equity
lunch/week	$47	Yes ☐ No ☑	
Netflix	$9.95	Yes ☑ No ☐	love movies!
gym fee	$89	Yes ☑ No ☐	health, energy, sanity
new shoes	$68	Yes ☐ No ☑	

| savings | $200 | Yes ✔ No ☐ | emergency cushion |
| plane ticket | $368 | Yes ✔ No ☐ | visiting best friend |

As you can see now, the point is not self-torture, but clarity. This book is about setting priorities, and when you live and spend contrary to what you value—you don't end up with the life you want.

A mundane example is what happens to a lot of people when they go into CVS, Duane Reade, Walgreens, or some other convenience store. You go in wanting toothpaste, and you leave having spent thirty dollars on half a dozen other things. (I've often wondered what happens to us in those stores. Are we overcome by the desperate need for cold medicine and hair conditioner? Supersize bags of Pepperidge Farm Goldfish?)

Anyway, thirty bucks may not seem like a big deal, but what's significant is how easy it is to spend money on lots of stuff . . . but nothing in particular. Clarifying where your money goes each month not only illuminates these financial black holes so you can retrieve your runaway cash, it also allows you to use that money to make happier choices. Just as you can spend money in such a way that it keeps you jogging on the competitive consumption treadmill, you can use your money to buy your way off it by investing in the things that enhance quality of life: your relationships, your health and well-being, new and stimulating experiences—all of which and more we'll talk about as the book unfolds.

Now, in order to get your finances really in sync with your happiness, it helps to master a few basic money management skills—which is what the next chapter is all about.

3

Take Financial Control

We can tell our values by looking
at our checkbook stubs.

—*Gloria Steinem*

N ow for a short chapter on how to manage your money.
If you'll allow me to make an educated guess, I'd bet
that right now you're probably thinking one of two things.
Either (1) You're interested in taking some of the steps toward
investing in greater happiness, but you're not sure where the
money is supposed to come from—since most of your income is
committed to the life you have now. Or (2) You find these ideas
compelling, but not compelling enough to change your habits,
because you secretly know that you'll be able to afford the material lifestyle you want, plus the happiness you need—*as soon
as you're making more money.*

Although they sound different, both of these misguided
ideas stem from the same fantasy: that what you need to be

happy depends on having more money, preferably a lot more than you have now. But if you're hoping that this is the part where I tell you how you're going to get rich *and* be happy, you'll have to pick up another book.

More money is nice. I know plenty of people who have attained a certain income level and lifestyle—and they enjoy the perks and privileges that greater wealth can buy. But the happiest people I know, well-off or not, have an innate sense of how to manage and spend their money so that it enriches their lives. That's what this chapter is about: acquiring better money management skills—the better to invest in a happier life with, my dear.

SMART PEOPLE DON'T FINISH RICH

You don't want to make the mistake countless Americans are making as we speak—and that is, waiting for wealth to waltz into their lives. According to a 2003 Gallup poll, about a third of Americans said they expected to be rich at some point—and 51 percent of people with incomes of $75,000-plus believed they definitely would be rich. And yet, according to Thomas A. DiPrete, chairman of the sociology department at Columbia University, most people don't even have a realistic idea of what "rich" means. For example, in that same Gallup poll, the median estimate was that earning about $120,000 a year would qualify as rich; only 8 percent of people said they'd need $1 million a year to consider themselves rich.

It's strange to think that, in a country that seems obsessed with wealth, we wouldn't have a clearer idea of how much "rich" was worth. But perhaps it's just as well, because the odds are that most people never will be much richer than they are right now. DiPrete analyzed national income data going back to 1968 to gauge how likely it was that people would significantly increase their income level within their lifetimes (never mind get rich). The answer was: not very likely. Someone earning $120,000 today, he found, has only a 19 percent chance of making $340,000 within the next fifteen years. For most of us, the odds of ever reaching the million-dollar threshold are depressingly low, despite what we see on TV.

So postponing your hopes and dreams—and happiness—because you're waiting for more money not only sets you up for disappointment, it prevents you from seizing the joy that can be yours with the money you have right now.

> **They always say time changes things, but you actually have to change them yourself.**   —*Andy Warhol*

I understand the frustrating sense that it might be impossible for you to invest in a happier life because it's already a struggle to pay your bills for the life you have. Some people, I agree, live between a rock and a genuine hard place financially. Others rely on the "I'm so stuck" excuse so they don't have to roll up their sleeves and take any action. I can't say where you stand, but I can tell you this: No matter what boat they are in, people are often surprised by how profoundly their lives improve when they master a few basic financial skills. I'm not talking about learning how to run Goldman Sachs. Simply strengthening your money management repertoire not only increases the control you have over your financial life—it will enable you to make all these happiness investments a reality, not just a cute metaphor in a book you once read.

GET A PLAN, STAN

As you may have noticed, the number of books, magazines, Web sites, and blogs devoted to personal finance could fill a black hole. Fortunately, in order to move your money habits in a happier direction right now, all you need to start is a basic blueprint for spending and saving.

I say "to start" for a reason. Unless you're a natural-born money manager, these skills take a while to develop—because they require that you rethink, revise, and ultimately reject some of your less fruitful money habits. The particular plan I'm about to share with you offers an easy-to-use set of guidelines to help you make substantive changes in how you think and behave financially with regard to your priorities. It's called the 60% Solution, and it outlines a series of spending and saving targets that will help you create order out of financial chaos. Again, this is more like a financial floor plan than detailed building instructions: It's meant to provide a structure you can work with according to your own lifestyle and goals. You may not hit every target, but by aiming for them you'll soon experience a major shift in your financial well-being that will make it easier for you to put your money where your happiness is.

This plan is short and deceptively simple, but it works—my editor Richard Jenkins invented it out of his own frustration with trying to keep his family finances in order. But if you can work with it as you go through this book, you will be stunned by how much more life you can get for your money.

THE 60% SOLUTION: COVERING THE BASICS

The first part of the 60% Solution addresses the 60 percent of your income that ideally should cover your essential or committed expenses. In other words, you want to get your basic living costs—which include your rent or mortgage, utility bills, car or commuting costs, taxes, groceries, tuition, child care, insurance, tithing or charitable donations, and so on—to equal about 60 percent of your gross, or pre-tax, income. Retirement, debt, and savings are separate; we'll get to those in a moment. Right now focus on what your most essential expenditures are—they are different for everyone. Dining out is probably not an essential expense; daily medication is; your Saturday night babysitter might be; books, music downloads, and other sorts of entertainment are not—they'll go into your Fun category, which I also address below. Clothing and gifts count as more irregular expenses, and they're also in a separate category.

Let's look at some monthly figures. If you earn, say, $4,000 a month gross, you would aim to keep your committed costs down to $2,400 a month. (I explain later why we use gross figures instead of net.)

Try it out right here. Get a piece of paper and jot down your gross monthly income. Now list below all the committed expenses you have each month and total them (Note: There are some blank spaces where you can add your own essential expenses):

_____ Taxes (check your pay stub)

_____ Health insurance withholdings/payments (ditto)

_____ Mortgage/rent

_____ Car payment

_____ Car insurance

_____ Tuition

_____ Charitable giving

_____ Child care

_____ Gas

_____ Phone

_____ Cell phone

_____ Heat

_____ Electricity

_____ Water

_____ Groceries

_____ Other [list here]

_____ Other

_____ Other

_____ **TOTAL**

Now subtract the total amount of your basic expenses from your monthly gross and calculate what percentage of your income is going toward your basic cost of living. It's probably more than 60 percent.

Taxes alone may take up 20 to 30 percent of your gross income—and you haven't even gotten to birthday gifts, holiday travel, retirement. But we're not done yet. Remember that we're working with targets here, so it's important to read through the whole plan; I answer the most common questions about it below.

Now comes the good part.

SAVING IN ORDER TO SPEND

Every month, without fail, there are always a bunch of unexpected expenditures that crop up—and they always seem to eat up exactly whatever extra money is lying around in your bank account. In the worst case—which also happens without fail, a couple of times a year—you don't have the money and you have to put those bigger outlays on your credit card. This system is specifically designed to help you cope with those constant cash drains.

Let's look at the remaining 40 percent of your monthly income, which we'll divide into four "buckets." Although this will appear to be an elaborate savings plan—it's a lot more useful (and accurate) if you think of it as a saving-to-spend plan.

- **BUCKET #1:** Ideally, you next should set aside 10 percent of your gross income each month for short-term, irregular expenses. Using the current example, that would be about $400 a month. This is the amount that you'll budget for the expenses life throws at you from time to time, like your cousin's wedding, that recent car repair, or the prescription your insurance wouldn't cover. These expenditures may be unexpected, but they are an inevitable part of life—so setting aside a regular amount of money each month to cover them is an effortless way to slash financial stress and boost your financial sanity.

- **BUCKET #2:** Same idea—set aside 10 percent per month to cover long-term expenses that you know are just over the horizon: the kids' braces; replacing the water heater; taking a vacation. These are expenses you can and should plan for—because they too are inevitable, and you don't want to get knocked silly when the time comes to replace your roof or your car and you haven't planned for it.

- **BUCKET #3:** The third 10-percent chunk goes toward retirement. Period. Don't argue with me, people, just aim to save 10 percent for your future—at the very least. More on that in chapter 9.

- **BUCKET #4:** The last chunk is what you should allocate for fun, frivolous, spontaneous expenses—anything from movies to M&M's, if that's your poison. This last category may sound superfluous, but in many ways it's the spoonful of sugar that makes the whole 60% Solution— or any spending system—work. And, hey, it fits in nicely with the aims of this book! You must invest a small but

steady part of your income for regular happiness supplements so you never feel like you're financially
deprived or, worse, on a budget. Luckily, you'll be
treated to a whole chapter on the importance of investing in fun later on—and you'll see why you need this 10
percent.

A Few FAQs

· **How do I decide what my committed expenses are?**
Think of your committed expenses as what's absolutely
necessary for you to live—or what you're committed to.
You may not need a gym membership to survive and
your daughter may not need clarinet lessons, but if it's
vital to your sanity or soul (or hers), it's a committed
expense. Cable, Internet, cell phone, Netflix—we all get
accustomed to thinking of certain expenses as neces-
saries, but if you're looking for ways to cut back, you can
always decide that some things are in fact expendable.

· **What category does debt fall into?** The way to think
about debt in terms of this spending plan is that it is *not*
a committed expense. If you're paying back credit card
debt, for example, you can use the 10 percent you'd normally set aside for future expenses for that. And/or you
can use 5 percent of the money that would go toward retirement and 5 percent of your fun money—until it's all
paid off. It depends on how much debt you have and
how aggressive you want to be. The 60% Solution is
pretty flexible; you don't have to stop saving to get out of

debt, but paying it back should be a priority. I address how to get out of debt in chapter 7, because the joy of being debt-free is an essential part of your happiness portfolio.

· **There's no way I can meet those targets. What should I do?** Adjust the numbers according to what's possible for you. Setting aside even 2 percent in each of the spending buckets is better than nothing. As you start to gain a sense of mastery over your finances, you will find it's easier to put more toward these targets than you thought.

· **Do I *have* to use my gross income as the basis for these calculations?** Yes. By using figures based on your gross income, you're more likely to cover all your expenses and make swifter progress toward your goals. If you need to start by taking baby steps, you can work from your net income. I know it's easier, in some ways, because that's how most people get paid. But try to work from your gross.

· **Where is the category for happiness?** Good question! You'll be funding the sectors of your happiness portfolio from all the various buckets of this spending plan—including your committed expenses (because I hope you'll be committed to being happy). In other words, investing in a so-called happiness portfolio isn't a separate category; it should and will become woven into many areas of your life, as you'll see in the coming chapters. Thus, you're not just putting 10 percent aside for the future, you're putting it aside for a happier future. When you map out your committed expenses, you'll begin to give more weight to those that yield a bigger happiness dividend. Instead of thinking you can skimp on your fun money, you'll realize that every dime you spend on fun is a valuable investment in your overall joie de vivre.

PUTTING YOUR MONEY PLAN TO WORK

It may be tempting to read through a fairly simple financial plan like this one and decide to ignore it. It seems too easy: 10 percent here, 10 percent there—how is that going to make any difference to your bottom line, never mind increase your happiness?

> **There is no security on earth, there is only opportunity.**
> —*Douglas MacArthur*

My advice is to sit down with a calculator and continue experimenting with the 60% Solution, seeing how it might apply to your own situation. Wouldn't it set your mind at ease to know you had a little money socked away for rainy-day expenses? Wouldn't you enjoy life more if you had some frivolous money to spend each month, guilt-free? In order to get the most out of this book, you'll find yourself reevaluating certain financial choices in favor of happiness—and this money management system is the tool you need.

SPOT YOUR BAD MONEY HABITS

This book is a guide to honing your financial self-awareness as well as investing in happiness. Now that you are getting a firmer grip on your finances, another good exercise is learning to find your financial blind spots. How can you enjoy greater happiness with your money until you rout out some bad habits? Everyone has at least one. Like the Walgreens example in the last chapter (remember the Goldfish!), your blind spot is simply the area in which you spend more money than you realized on stuff that's not that important to you. You'll know you've hit a blind spot when you scrutinize your monthly expenses and a strange, extravagant spending pattern will appear, and your reaction will be, "Wow, I spent this much on *that*?"

Here are some classic blind spots:

- **The Splurger:** It's not how often you buy, it's how much you spend when you do. You're the gal with the $300 boots; you're the guy with the fully loaded car—or vice versa. You think of yourself as fiscally responsible because you've never gotten a late fee on a bill, and little indulgences don't tempt you. You'll take the bus before you'll take a cab. But you're a sucker for anything with a designer label.

- **Random Spender:** You get your credit card bill and you're shocked, shocked! You think: "I *couldn't* have spent $350 this month, because I know for certain I only spent $25 on Joe's birthday and $15 on a new printer cable, and—oh, right, $10 on a new umbrella—and then there was that jacket, but it was on sale for $19.99 . . ." And by the time you run down the itemized list, you still can't believe how it added up to $350! But it did.

· **Friend Spending:** Sometimes, investing in your social network is a powerful source of happiness. But like any other pleasure, it can get out of hand. How can something that feels so good possibly be the source of real financial problems? If this is your Achilles' heel, look no farther than all the lunches, brunches, dinners, movies, coffees, drinks, birthdays, weddings, showers, trips, and getaways that crowd your calendar and drain the cash right out of your bank account.

· **Discount Delusions:** You never pay full price, you know every outlet store in a ninety-mile range, you shop only at Costco, Sam's Club, and Wal-Mart, and "bulk" is your middle name. Sadly, it's just as easy—maybe even easier—to overspend on unnecessaries that you justify with the excuse "But it was so cheap!" Unfortunately, the math of spending on two-for-the-price-of-one, when you didn't need either one to begin with, never adds up.

Those are just four common blind spots; your own may be different, but uncovering yours will offer some useful lessons about the misguided ways you spend. Again, these exercises aren't designed to make you feel guilty, but to help you develop greater financial awareness and control—because then you can start making conscious trade-offs in order to spend less on stuff and more on living and enjoying life.

YOU *CAN* AFFORD TO BE HAPPY

When I say trade-off, what I mean is learning to apply more of a cost-benefit analysis to all your quality-of-life decisions. You make calculations like this every day, but now you'll be doing more of them in order to make some of the happiness investments you're reading about. Here are some examples of how doing a simple cost-benefit analysis can enhance your everyday life:

- One very busy lawyer I know gets all her laundry and dry cleaning picked up and dropped off at her home each week. It's worth every dime for her to pay extra for these services so she has more free time.
- Conversely, let's say you want to go out with your spouse this weekend, but the cost of babysitting seems exorbitant. With the amount of money you'd save by handwashing a few sweaters instead of dry-cleaning them, you'd have your babysitting money.
- Or: Instead of buying a new car and living with a $300 car payment every month for the next five years, what about using your savings to buy a "pre-owned vehicle"— and sock away the $300 a month toward your dream tour of Alaska, getting out of debt, or some other happier investment?
- Everyone needs a work wardrobe, but how much of your hard-earned money do you really want to commit to clothing, shoes, and accessories? What about shopping

online or at a consignment shop and using some of the money you save to attend a friend's wedding or redecorate your living room?

- Let's say you love to cook. You don't have to take a $3,500 gourmet tour of Tuscany to get more out of your hobby. Dump your least favorite magazine and spend the money on a subscription to *Food & Wine* or *Cooks Illustrated* or some other publication that inspires you. Pare down your cell phone splurges (text messages, wallpaper, ringtones) and spring for the deluxe cable deal so you can enjoy all those cooking shows.

These are painless ways to refocus your financial decisions in favor of a happier, richer life—and you can see how using the 60% Solution can aid you in your quest. Maybe your work wardrobe has been one of your committed expenses—except that now you realize you'd like to be more committed to building your collection of World War I model airplanes. Now you can use your growing financial control to shift the way you spend so that more of your money goes toward your priorities.

One of the ways I learned to stop spending so much on eating out was by doing a series of cost-benefit analyses—on everything from breakfast to lunch to drinks and snacks to dinner. Cutting back on dinners out was easy because the tab for eating at a restaurant even twice a week can add up to the equivalent of one plane ticket per month—and I'd rather have the opportunity to travel than consume a parade of overpriced pasta dishes. But these ongoing financial calculations also helped me cut back on the smaller meals I'd grab on the go, because frankly there are a dozen ways I'd rather spend my money than on a bunch of forgettable sandwiches.

> **People are about as happy as they make up their minds to be.** —*Abraham Lincoln*

That doesn't mean I renounced eating out. I just became a lot more conscious about where, when, and why I spent that money—always making sure that when I did, I took it as a delicious chance to catch up with a friend or spend time with my husband (both of which are big stocks in my own happiness portfolio).

I realize that this is a quick overview of a complex topic, but we'll continue to work on different aspects of your personal finances—and how they intersect with your personal happiness—throughout the book. Next on the docket is learning to manage another big expenditure: time.

4

Buy Yourself
More Time

Lost time is never found again.

—Benjamin Franklin

To hear people talk about it, you would think everyone
knows how valuable their time is. "Time is money," people
often say, and in fact we use many of the same words for time as
we do for cash. We say that doing X "saved me time" or doing Y
"was worth the time." We talk about spending time, wasting
time, investing time, and above all not having enough time.

The only hitch is that many of us tend to forget that time is a
commodity far more priceless than money. Cash may be replace-
able, but time is not. You can't beg, borrow, steal, or manufacture
more time. There are no ATM time-dispensing machines, no
time credit cards (you may have noticed).

All you have is what you hold in your hands each day. If you
knew how big or small your personal chunk of time was—if you

could check the balance in your personal time account online—that would change many of the decisions you make about how you spend your time. Alas, no one can ever know how many hours, days, or weeks he or she is entitled to—and that's what makes investing as much of your time as you can in the life you want right now all the more essential.

You can't save tonight and hope to spend it next month, right? But you can increase the amount of time you have to spend each day by using your money to "buy" more of it.

A WRINKLE IN TIME

Unfortunately, people feel even more strapped for time than they do for money. "There's not enough time!" is the collective wail of our age. At first glance that seems to be true. Americans work long hours on top of even longer commutes. We spend an average of seventy-two minutes a day commuting. Our days are stuffed with obligations, errands, commitments, and to-do lists; and we're increasingly equipped with gadgets—cell phones, PDAs, pagers, home PCs—that are supposed to save us time but instead end up siphoning off more of the time we have. No wonder people gripe, "My time is not my own." We're so pressed that many of us don't even take the time off from work that we're entitled to. According to the Travel Industry Association, the annual American vacation has gotten shorter—about 4.5 days on average—and in 2005 employees left a total of 421 million vacation days untouched at the end of the year.

The cumulative effect of nearly two centuries of increased

industrialization has encouraged most people to trade their time primarily for money, a theme explored by journalist Carl Honore in his book *In Praise of Slowness*. More time working means more money earned, which means more purchasing power. You feel deprived of time because on one level you are—you've traded it for stuff. But on another level this trade-off has contributed to a strange sort of amnesia: We forget that our time still belongs to us. Your time *is* your own, and just as you've traded your hours and days for cash, it's also possible to reverse the equation so you can put more of your time toward the kind of life you want.

Which brings us to the question: *How can you buy yourself more time?*

You couldn't be asking at a better moment. Modern life has become so hectic, so frantic, so time-squeezed that millions of people around the world, literally, are seeking solutions to the time crunch—on the personal front, but especially when it comes to our professional lives. The meaning of that old saying "Time is money" is shifting as more people start to realize, Hey, time *is* money—and all this *time* I'm spending getting *money* is depleting the hours I could be spending on other things. In this chapter I'll focus first on work, the biggest of our time trades, and then examine some of the time traps that can snare your downtime, too.

THE SLOW MOVEMENT OF TIME

Even at the upper echelons of corporate America, there's a big shift in favor of balancing work and private time.

In 2005, when *Fortune* magazine polled top U.S. executives about the work-time imbalance:

- 64 percent said at this stage in their lives they would take more time over money.
- 80 percent of those surveyed said that they were somewhat or very comfortable talking to their bosses about "balancing work and the things outside work that are important to me."
- Fully 98 percent of executives said they were "sympathetic to requests from their own reports for a better work-life balance."

> **Time is the coin of your life. It is the only coin you have, and only you can determine how it will be spent. Be careful lest you let other people spend it for you.** —*Carl Sandburg*

Compared to a decade ago, there are a wider variety of time-friendly work policies available—and a growing body of research to back up the notion that giving workers nontraditional schedules doesn't have to hurt a company's bottom line. Moreover, the extraordinary advances in technology are making it possible for employees to negotiate much more flexible work arrangements. For example:

- job sharing
- flex time (e.g., working forty hours, but not on a rigid nine-to-five schedule)
- shorter work weeks

- telecommuting (e.g., working from home or from different locations)
- trading a raise or a bonus for extra vacation time or longer weekends
- working part-time and living on less
- quality-of-life increases (e.g., the company pays for your cell phone, car, commuter pass, gym membership, etc.)
- stepping off the "fast track" (e.g., not vying for a promotion or a raise in order to keep work levels manageable)

Of course, the big question for most people is: "Can I afford a time-friendly work schedule—financially and professionally?"

The answer may surprise you.

When Sylvia, twenty-eight, and Carmi, thirty-five, started a job-share arrangement at their software company a couple of years ago, at first they were amazed that they'd finagled the deal at all.

Carmi had been lobbying for years to go part-time, and her bosses simply refused. "They literally laughed at me," Carmi says. After she had her son, Carmi decided to take matters into her own hands. She quit and took a job as a consultant within the same company—basically showing her managers that she could still get her job done working even fewer hours. So when her consulting contract ended, the company was willing to give her the job share with her coworker Sylvia, working just thirty-two hours.

Carmi did have to take a pay cut, but because she and her husband, a stay-at-home dad, had already scaled back while she was consulting, the financial shift wasn't that onerous. It was more difficult for Sylvia, who was taking courses in order to get into medical school, and could work only two days a week. "I had to take a huge pay cut," Sylvia says, admitting that it's been hard to trade nice haircuts and evenings out with friends for the more "PB&J lifestyle of a student."

It's difficult for most of us to imagine living with a drop in income without having a twinge of panic, or a fear of deprivation, but both Carmi and Sylvia focused on the fact that they were trading that extra income in order to gain more hours for other aspects of life. It was far more important to Sylvia to know that she was finally making the leap out of a career in computers and into medicine than it was to keep earning a fat paycheck. Likewise, Carmi desperately wanted to have more time for her family, but also for her fiction-writing—which until that point she had squeezed in during her bus ride to work.

People make similar investment calculations all the time, but usually going the other way. You might say to yourself: When I earn more money, then I can afford a bigger mortgage, a better car, a vacation in the Bahamas, a new deck on my house. And that's fine, *if that's how you want to invest your time.* There's nothing wrong with trading your time for income, benefits, and home improvements—these can also contribute to your happiness. The trouble arises when you reach a point of diminishing returns, and the amount of time and energy it takes to maintain a certain lifestyle is no longer worth the financial gain.

These calculations are intensely personal. If you want to buy a bigger house, a new car, or take that vacation in the Bahamas, then you may make a different time-versus-money calculation.

You may decide to go for a promotion, ask for a raise, or work overtime in order to afford those things. But many exhausted, frustrated Americans are looking around and saying: Wait a minute, there's got to be a more satisfying way.

> **There is only one success—to be able to spend your life in your own way.** —*Christopher Morley*

KNOW THE VALUE OF YOUR TIME

How can you make some of these calculations in your own life? Start by assessing the hidden costs of the work you do. When Carmi decided to forgo a full-time paycheck, for example, she had to think about how much she was getting paid for *all* the work she was doing. Like most people, she knew that her forty-hour week was really more like fifty or sixty hours—or more, when a big project was due. In addition, she spent about ten hours a week commuting and a few hours doing catch-up on weekends. When you start to plug all the numbers into this equation, your paycheck looks a lot smaller—especially when you deduct work-related costs from your salary.

Let's say Carmi was earning $65,000 in her full-time job. Her gross weekly paycheck was about $1,354—or about $34 an hour, before taxes. Now let's add in some of those work-related time costs.

In reality she was working more like fifty hours a week,

which equals $27 an hour, before taxes. From that she could also deduct the following expenses:

- buying lunch = $35/week
- buying coffee and snacks = $25/week
- paying for day care = $0 (her husband takes care of their son)
- paying for the purchase and maintenance of a work wardrobe = $30/week (Carmi isn't a fashionista)
- commuting costs = $42/week

So when you subtract the approximately $132 per week from her base salary, Carmi's hourly wage drops to $24 an hour—and that still doesn't take into account her taxes and other withholdings. So you can see how Carmi realized that by switching to a job-share arrangement, she'd be officially working fewer hours—and yet the pay she would get wouldn't be much less than what she'd been earning full-time, when everything else was factored in. "When I was working full-time, a 45-hour week meant I'd probably be working more like 60 hours," Carmi says. "Now I work 32 hours a week—and I get paid for 32 hours a week—but I rarely have to work more than that."

This is not to say you can afford to quit your full-time job, but by doing a similar set of reckonings in your own life, you'll get a new perspective on how much you're really getting paid for all the time you spend. You can find an even more detailed version of this time-versus-income exercise in *Your Money or Your Life*, by Joe Dominguez and Vicki Robin, the book that revolutionized how many people evaluate their time and money. I strongly recommend reading it. (You also can learn more about related topics at www.simpleliving.net.)

YOUR TIME, YOUR LIFE

Just as we examined your cash flow so you could get a better grip on where your money is going, now we'll do the same with the time you'd like to call your own.

A couple of years ago, two professors at the London Business School were teaching a course on corporate strategies and how companies could better achieve their aims through a smarter use of their own resources. They developed an exercise to help the business students analyze a company's performance, and what they found was that outside the class, students were applying this framework to their own lives—specifically how they spent or invested their time.

So let's try doing a similar analysis of your time-spending habits: You have approximately 112 waking hours in each week; how do you spend the hours when you're not working? Are you investing your personal, disposable time in ways that maximize your greatest happiness?

EXERCISE
Keeping Time

What you'll need: some paper, a pen, and your schedule, calendar, or PDA. If last week was unusual (if you were on vacation or blitzed at work), pick a week that reflects your typical schedule. Time required: about 15 minutes.

1. On one piece of paper make two columns. In the first, list your top ten personal values or priorities—but don't get too bogged down in particulars. Remember: These exercises should be fast and fun, and this one is meant to give you an overview of where your time goes. So for now, limit your list to ten priorities, but be as specific as you can about each one. Rather than writing down "family," state what it is about family that's a priority for you: for example, "spending time with my kids," "visiting my mom." If you value "working hard," specify in what way: for example, "working hard so I can get a great bonus."

2. Don't censor yourself. These are *your* priorities, your values, right now. Rising through the ranks of your company is just as valid as helping your child pass algebra this year—or meditating more often.

3. Now look at your calendar and review your week, and in the second column write down the number of hours you devoted to each item in the first column that week. If you're not sure, ballpark it. (Hint: This is easiest if you take one of your priorities and scan each day to see how much time you spent on it; ditto for the next priority.)

As a reality check, tally up the number of hours you spent on these various priorities to make sure you end up with less than 112. Most of us need time to eat, watch TV, commute, run errands, read the paper, and so on.

Most of us think we have a pretty good idea about where our time goes—and most of us cling to the belief that we're doing our best, spending as much time as we can on what's important to us. Meanwhile, without doing the math on where your hours really go, it's easy to keep deluding yourself about the truth. Someone might ask you: "How often do you work out?" You might say, "Oh, a couple of times a week," even though your calendar would laugh at you. But if working out is really a priority for you, or if spending time with your nieces and nephews really makes you happy, then it should show up in the time inventory you did, not just in your imagination. On the other hand, if how you allot your time doesn't match your priorities, this exercise will reveal where your time is getting lost:

- You can see which priorities get the most of your time, and which aren't getting enough.
- You can weigh whether you'd like to make some changes; that is, redistribute your time.
- You can refine the *sort* of time certain priorities may require.

When I did this exercise, two of my core values—getting exercise and spending time talking to or visiting my family—got zero hours and about one hour of my week, respectively. My husband got about twenty waking hours; work got close to forty;

friends about twelve (including phone calls); doing things for fun and cultural enrichment also got about twelve.

The glaring omission here was the paltry amount of time I was giving to two aspects of my life that really do make me enormously happy—physical activity and family connection. (And I'm embarrassed to admit that I forgot to include my spiritual life here entirely.)

The other revelation for me was, although I often feel that I don't spend enough time with my husband—I realized that the problem wasn't the number of hours we were spending together, it was what we were doing with our time. Rather than hanging out at home, I realized that what I really loved was when the two of us would do things together—like seeing movies or visiting friends—and that I wanted to invest more in that direction.

LOOK OUT FOR TIME TRAPS

It's a lot easier to quantify your work time in financial terms, but the same investment rules apply when you want to take back your downtime. Let's use the classic example of what happens when you get stuck in a time trap.

Time traps are like sand traps. You back into them—and then have a heck of a time getting out. One example is joining something, like a book club, the PTA, the local Hornswogglers Association. I love groups. I've joined them; I've formed them. But sometimes you neglect to take into account what a certain commitment will cost you in terms of time.

"Will you host the potluck dinner?" is one of those fatal phrases that captures what I'm talking about.

You say sure—you're happy to host the potluck dinner—forgetting your time-life math and thinking that all it will require is an hour to make some macaroni and cheese, and then three or four hours when people come over for the dinner that night. You can take five hours out of your week, right?

But you've forgotten the two hours of phone calls to coordinate who's bringing dessert or chips or soda. You've forgotten that you'll have to shop for and actually cook the casserole. You've forgotten that you'll spend an hour cleaning the house beforehand, and more time handling other details. Fifteen hours later . . . you host the potluck.

We've all volunteered for some version of the potluck that became a fifteen-hour crater in the week, or committed to a project that ate an entire month. Sometimes these decisions may cost a lot of time, but what you gain—in terms of fun, camaraderie, satisfaction—is well worth the time you spent. The trick is knowing how to use money to regain some of that time (and reduce that frantic stress dance) when you most need it. The potluck example above gives a lot of insight into ways you might invest your money to free up your time. You might:

- order pizza or sandwiches from a deli instead of spending time cooking
- hire a housekeeper to straighten up instead of doing it yourself
- pay a babysitter to pick up the kids after school, so you can get organized

I realize how simplistic these solutions may sound—but how often do you give yourself the license to spend money in order to buy back your time—and increase your quality of life?

SPEND MORE TO HAVE MORE TIME

You'll find more ideas about how to save time and buy yourself peace of mind in chapter 8. Meanwhile, here are some specific ways you can invest your money in goods or services that will free up more time for yourself—and for the things in life that make you happiest.

- **Housecleaning:** Not everyone can afford a regular housekeeper, but even a monthly visit can free up a chunk of time that you can use for greater enjoyment in your own life. And P.S.: A professional cleaner will leave your house so spotless that you can probably get away with doing less housework for a week or two yourself.
- **Babysitting:** I know many couples who hesitate to splurge on a babysitter, but giving yourself and your mate the occasional breather and chance to reconnect— with each other, with your friends, with life in general— is one of the best ways to enrich your relationship. Contact your local colleges; many have inexpensive babysitting services. Or join a babysitting co-op in your area, where parents swap child-care time.
- **Professional Organizing:** Is there anything more time-consuming than clutter? You can almost count the number of fretful hours you waste in sporadic attempts

to cope with it all, or spend in a fruitless search for some receipt or memo or phone number. Hire someone to help. Try the National Association of Professional Organizers (www.napo.net) to find someone in your area. You don't have to spend $500 to make your place look like a Martha Stewart "model home," but for a reasonable sum you can have an organizer clear up one specific area—leaving you with a bonanza of tips, tricks, and skills that you can then apply to the rest of your home. (That's what I did!)

· **Chores:** Lawns and gardens and gutters—oh my! Many homeowners have been bitten by the DIY bug in recent years, but is that how you really want to spend your valuable downtime? If gardening and repairs bring you peace of mind, bully for you. But there's nothing wrong with giving your pioneer spirit a rest and calling to find out what the neighbor's teenager charges for doing basic chores. Doing laundry, grocery shopping, and errand-running are other duties you can farm out to gain more time.

· **Your Money:** Unless you love spreadsheets, there's no reason to tie up your time with paying bills and balancing accounts when a simple software program like Excel, Quicken, or Microsoft Money can help you do it all in just a few short minutes. And I mean *all:* Some software programs allow you to monitor your checking account, check your credit card spending, keep an eye on your 401(k), set up a basic budget, and plan your retirement. Or you can hire an accountant to help you manage these tasks. (I use software *and* I pay an accountant to do my taxes. The windfall of time I get for spending a little money for someone else's financial expertise is priceless to me.)

The point is to recognize that a relatively small expenditure of money can yield a substantial bonus of time—which you can then invest in your life.

Next, we turn to another great enricher: investing in yourself.

5

Invest in Yourself

Storybook happiness involves every form of
pleasant thumb-twiddling; true happiness involves
the full use of one's powers and talents.

—*John Gardner*

A chapter about investing in yourself may sound like I'm going to tell you to "follow your bliss"—or impart some amazing career advice. Luckily, it's not about either of those things.

It's about filling up a big tank of pink liquid.

In a recent paper, economists Liam Graham and Andrew Oswald put forth a new investment-based model of happiness, which suggests that people rely on a reservoir of well-being within themselves that they draw upon to sustain and enrich their lives. Oswald and Graham call this stash of good feeling "hedonic capital," and they unfurl a rather elaborate mathematical formula to demonstrate that your personal happiness can be stored, spent, and replenished—depending on what's going on in life: "Just as machines produce output, hedonic capital produces a flow of resources which might be termed hedonic energy," they write. "We posit that this energy can be used either to generate well-being today or to invest in hedonic capital to produce well-being in the future."

To put it a little more playfully, in one talk he gave, Dr. Oswald referred to one's personal reserve of happiness as "a big tank of pink liquid," making it sound almost like an internal source of hydrogen or some other fuel. And that's the idea: "I find it useful to imagine a tax on your well-being—let's say if you become ill or go through a divorce or get a pay cut," Dr. Oswald said when I spoke to him. "Then that big tank of pink liquid is the stuff you draw on to smooth the negative shock. You can draw on that over the years."

Dr. Oswald said he lacked the empirical data to say how, exactly, people might build up their store of pink liquid. But based on a growing body of research emerging from the field of positive psychology, it seems that when people focus on enriching themselves in various ways—by developing and exploring their strengths, abilities, goals, and passions—we do indeed add to that internal pool of well-being.

Unfortunately, for some people the idea of "investing" in themselves for anything other than professional reasons may feel frivolous, selfish, or maybe flat-out unnecessary. Many people give to themselves indirectly—by devoting their resources to their spouse, family, job, or community. Those ways of investing do yield big returns, as we'll explore in upcoming chapters, but they're not the same as nurturing the fundamental source of your own well-being. By giving yourself what you need to flourish and be whole and happy—whether that involves becoming a leader in your community, resolving to learn Italian before your next trip to Rome, or finally joining that knitting group—the greater gain is that you'll have more resources to put into all the other areas of life.

EXERCISE

Being Warren Buffett

First let's do a short exercise that illustrates what I mean by investing in yourself and why it's important.

You'll need five empty cups, mugs, or glasses (paper, plastic, whatever), five small pieces of paper or Post-its, and a pen. (Note: You'll be tempted to carry this out as a thought experiment, imagining yourself taking each step, etc. Don't. Get up and get some cups—the whole exercise will take you five minutes. If you're not in a place where you can procure some empty glasses, do it when you get home—but allow yourself the actual, physical experience.)

Fill one cup with water. Then place the remaining four empty cups in a row and label each one according to your top four priorities right now. Not the people or things you *wish* were important, but the areas where most of your time and energy are directed *right now*—into your job or career, your child, finishing the basement, being on the community board, your romantic relationship, or whatever your priorities may be.

Now pour some water from the first cup into each of

your priority cups, roughly approximating how much of your personal energy goes toward each of those things. It's fine to pour back and forth to adjust the amounts. Certain cups will end up with more water than others, and you can glean whatever insights you like from that. But this water experiment can be illuminating in other ways. Here are some questions to think about:

- Most people assume they're supposed to pour all the water from the main cup into their priority cups; did you? Or did you save some in the first cup?
- Did it occur to you that the main cup, full of water at the start, represents your whole self—your time, money, energy, focus, and spirit?
- Bearing that in mind, if you could pour some water back into the main cup, where would it come from? How much would you put back?
- Now write down on the last piece of paper how you might spend the water in the main cup: That is, if you invested more of your resources—your money, time, and energy—into you, what would you do?

GO WITH THE FLOW

On the face of it there would seem to be an endless number of choices for each person, a bounty of ways you might spend your money and other resources on yourself that could be considered an investment. How do you choose? Where do you begin? How do you know what would really enrich your life?

Mihaly Csikszentmihalyi, founder and director of the Quality of Life Research Institute at Claremont Graduate University in Chicago, is one of the foremost researchers in this field. What has made Dr. Csikszentmihalyi so well-known is his pioneering work on a phenomenon known as "flow." Flow is a state of total absorption in a particular activity, which, although it may be demanding or even stressful while you're engaged in it, afterward conveys a profound sense of satisfaction. When I spoke to him, Dr. Csikszentmihalyi (pronounced "check-sent-me-high") described these activities as "the optimal conjunction of work and play"—because they are both effortful and fun.

Every field—from psychology to economics to religion to fitness—has its own way of describing the uplifting experience of being immersed in an activity that's equal parts challenge and reward, but they all revolve around what Dr. Csikszentmihalyi calls "growth-producing, complex activities." Although that may sound like you need to sign up for an Outward Bound course, in the thousands of assessments and interviews that he and his team of researchers have conducted over the years, Dr. Csikszentmihalyi found that people can achieve this elevated state while doing almost anything. While he often uses rock-climbing as an example of an undertaking that can inspire great passion and focus—and deliver quite an achiever's high—being carried away by a good book is the most common way people enjoy the deeply satisfying experience of being immersed in a task that makes you feel more alive.

Thus reaping the benefits of flow is less about restricting

yourself to a certain menu of activities than tapping into the things that hold the most meaning for you, that stoke your excitement and turn you on. Ryan, a retiree who lives in El Paso, Texas, discovered this when a friend talked him into joining the local theater company. Although he'd done some acting when he was younger, many years had passed since Ryan, sixty-seven, had been part of a live theater production. "Suddenly I was learning lines, attending rehearsals, meeting people— I even ended up teaching an acting class at the community college."

Ryan also started spending a bit more to go out with a few of his theater friends, taking in other regional shows. "Even in El Paso, you have to keep up with the competition," he jokes. It wasn't the quiet retirement Ryan had envisioned. "If you had asked me when I moved here if I was looking for all this activity, I would have said no way. But the truth is, I feel more creative and fulfilled than I have in years," he says.

Like most people who tap into a passion or find an activity that makes them feel more alive, Ryan hardly notices the expenditures he makes in terms of time or money because the returns he's getting far outweigh any expense. In addition to attending theater and movie nights with his friends, he has joined a group that hosts a rotating series of potlucks, and he helped some local writers self-publish a book of screenplays. Paraphrasing a quote from one of his favorite movies, *The Cider House Rules*, Ryan says that what he's discovered isn't just a diversion, but a sense of purpose: "You have to be of use," he says. "It's remarkable how things fall into place when you decide to invest in yourself."

STRIVING VERSUS SLACKING

Why do people seem so satisfied by experiences that require substantial mental (and sometimes physical) effort? Because it appears that human beings crave experiences that push us to the limit of our skills and thus stretch our sense of who we are and what we're capable of. In Dr. Csikszentmihalyi's view, there is perhaps an inborn drive, "an experiential need" that's akin to the other basic human needs for food, warmth, and comfort—and which likewise contributes to people's optimal well-being.

Of course, people also demonstrate a remarkable need to watch TV and download silly videos, too. And while there is a time and a place for mindless entertainment, when choosing between the pleasant distraction of relaxing in front of your favorite sitcom lineup or an activity that's more engaging, there's no contest as to which investment will best supplement your store of happiness. While easy pleasures deliver short-term gratification, "in fact, the returns tend to decrease over time (i.e., we get bored and listless)," Dr. Csikszentmihalyi writes. "On the other hand, the effort spent in learning to play a guitar, or a new language or sport or in helping others, does tend to bring greater returns in the future—that is, we get more enjoyment from life as a result of learning new skills and perceiving new opportunities."

Don't stay in bed, unless you can make money in bed.

—*George Burns*

What Dr. Csikszentmihalyi's research shows is that by investing in more active "growth-producing" activities in all aspects of your life—

- at work
- at home
- in your relationship with your mate
- with your children
- for yourself

"you will feel more happy, more creative, more content, more alert and have higher self-esteem relative to your own baseline," he says.

This is supported by the research of Sonja Lyubomirsky, a psychologist at the University of California, Riverside, and colleagues, who have found that "intentional activities" seem to have a substantial impact on long-term well-being, compared to just changing or improving your circumstances. In an article called "Pursuing Happiness: The Architecture of Sustainable Change," Dr. Lyubomirsky reports that when she and her associates studied college students who chose to pursue certain personal goals over the course of a semester, those who made the most progress toward or attained their goals showed the most increase in well-being—even three years later.

Dr. Lyubomirsky doesn't believe people's greater satisfaction comes from the rosy glow of success. Rather, investing in what she calls a self-generated goal leads to "accumulations of daily positive experiences" as you make progress or simply learn new skills.

Making a conscious investment in yourself also tends to create a sort of upward spiral of enjoyment as you allow yourself to expand and explore. This was the experience of Beth, forty-one, when she decided to go back to school to learn massage therapy after she was laid off from her job at the Bureau of Land Management in Oregon.

Some years before, her brother had died of AIDS, and therapeutic massage was one of the few things that brought him relief, she says. Since then she'd felt drawn to the idea of being a licensed massage therapist herself, in order to work with AIDS patients. The only trouble was that going back to school for a year would require her family's patience, plus a tremendous investment of both time and money until she could begin practicing.

In addition to borrowing nearly $10,000 in student loans, Beth accepted her in-laws' offer to cover some of her school expenses—but even with this support, Beth and her family had to live on less than half of their previous household income. Beth often felt frazzled with guilt and tried to make up for the fact that she was putting herself first. "I thought I had to be super student *and* super mother. So the first quarter I was really nose-to-the-grindstone. I couldn't allow myself any free time. If I wasn't studying I was cleaning house, playing with my daughter, or making sure dinner was ready."

Fortunately, Beth wasn't far into her program when she realized that her risky investment was paying off. She loved studying anatomy and physiology, and she seemed to have a natural talent for massage. As she adjusted to student life, it dawned on

her that pursuing a way of life she found exciting and meaningful wasn't just a good idea—it was an investment in herself that
was long overdue. After all, she had happily supported her husband when he was studying to be an architect. "The whole prior
decade, my focus was totally on helping him get through school,
setting up his career," she says. "Not that I didn't benefit from
that, but the focus of my thirties was on my husband and my
daughter. So I decided that it was okay for me to take time for
myself, to help myself do the things that I wanted."

THE GOOD LIFE STARTS HERE

Obviously Beth embarked on a pretty major investment in
herself—and a successful one—but not every self-investment
has to take up a lot of time, nor does it require a major life
change. In fact, what I like best about Beth's story is what happened next. Midway through her program, Beth turned forty
and decided to embark on "the Year of Me"—in which she found
all kinds of ways to explore and enjoy herself, from swimming
to sunbathing nude in the backyard ("My husband was a little
surprised," she says) to roller-skating, believe it or not. Re-
connecting to a more active, physical enjoyment of life became
Beth's "Year of Me" theme—and that's where she decided to invest more of her time, energy, and money.

"It's been a big change in how I spend my monthly 'fun
money,' " she says, referring to her portion of the household
budget. "My money is going almost exclusively toward paying

for entry fees or the equipment I might need," she says. "I just decided that there's so much focus on the future and saving for retirement, but I'm working so hard on having a good life—and part of having a good life is enjoying it now."

And enjoying it she is: "This roller-skating thing is purely for me—the goofy experience of going to the roller rink and watching all the dorky fourteen-year-old boys who hang out there. But I'm learning from those kids. They take such pleasure in trying new moves, even if they wipe out. I think it's really healthy, mentally and physically, to try out something that is foreign and fun, to challenge yourself in all ways."

In some ways it may be easier to imagine spending $500 for a seminar that will help you get a raise and a promotion. Then you can measure the "success" of your investment in terms of how your career progresses. Investing in yourself requires doing a different sort of math, looking for gains in your own sense of well-being, self-esteem, and enjoyment in life. In the following section I'll describe a few basic steps that will enable you to start investing more in this key sector of your own portfolio, and building up that tank of pink liquid.

YOU'RE ALONE ON THE ISLAND: WHAT DO YOU *REALLY* WANT TO DO?

As you read through this section, keep a piece of paper handy so you can jot down ideas as they strike you. Don't be too restrictive or reality-based at this point; you just want to generate some possibilities. Forget about how much time you do or don't have, whether you'll be any good at Ultimate Frisbee at your age—or whether you have the money to do any of these things (or if your friends will think you're nuts). Think back to those five glasses, and how much you give to the different parts of your life. Here's a step-by-step guide to putting some of that energy back into you.

Step 1: Find What You Like to Do

In case you don't have a repertoire of activities you plan to invest in right now—and many people don't—"At first put the emphasis on something that you would really like to do, or always wanted to do when you were a child but never did," says Dr. Csikszentmihalyi. Start by making a list of long-standing interests. Maybe you'd like to learn how to:

- pick stocks
- roll sushi
- design a Web site
- take salsa lessons
- build a bookcase
- speak comfortably in public
- do a podcast
- study the civil rights movement
- understand supply-side economics
- bake bread

Okay, I admit that's the stuff I'd like to learn. But you get the idea. Write down your own list and then pick at least one thing you have a genuine interest in exploring, and plan how you might begin to do so.

Or find new ways to enjoy an old pastime. You may never again be a drummer in the hottest garage band in your town, for example, but you can still fool around with friends, get back into the indie music scene—explore a new facet of music by teaching or composing or downloading like a madman. Dig up one old talent of yours, dust it off, and just see what happens. You know your skills better than I do, so I won't brainstorm on your behalf—but if nothing leaps to mind, do take a few minutes to revisit the hobbies of years past to remind yourself of things you might love to have in your life again.

> **Your vision will become clear only when you can look into your own heart. Who looks outside, dreams; who looks inside, awakes.**   —*Carl Jung*

Step 2: Let Your Curiosity Be Your Guide

Or maybe you're in the mood for something completely different. Kate Hanley, creator of MsMindbody.com, an inspirational Web site that focuses on small ways to invest in your health and well-being, points out that people often say, "If I had more time, I would . . ." She recommends paying attention to the moments when you find those words crossing your own lips. Maybe it's when a headline on a grocery store magazine catches your eye or a friend describes her wacky aunt's skydiving adventures—and something piques your curiosity.

"When you feel that spark inside yourself, respond," Hanley says.

In order to open yourself up to new experiences, earmark a little money each week for an adventure or two:

- Attend an open-mike comedy night.
- Check out a band you've never heard of.
- Try hypnosis.
- Volunteer for an upcoming food drive.
- Attend a live performance of . . . anything (theater, dance, multimedia).
- Sign up for a bike-a-thon.
- Join a march, rally, or letter-writing campaign for a cause you find compelling.
- Get a makeover.
- Explore a new restaurant.
- Attend a lecture.
- Hire someone to feng shui your "space."

Step 3: Pay Attention to What Feels Right

How do you know when you've found a pursuit that would make for a rewarding self-investment? "It's not rocket science," says Dr. Csikszentmihalyi. "It's a question of being aware of your own feelings and calculating the consequences of what you're doing." There will always be the temptation to stick with the routine that's most familiar or to remain a couch potato. "This is true for most adults—we take the easy way out too often," Dr. Csikszentmihalyi says. "I understand that we all need to relax, but if you do it too much, you get sucked into a kind of spiral of lassitude that ends up taking away the real joy of living."

To combat the human tendency to slide down the path of least resistance yet again, pay attention to which activities do feel the best, the most stimulating, the most enjoyable to you— and make a conscious effort to invest more in those. Then, says Dr. Csikszentmihalyi, let the momentum build naturally from there.

To get yourself going, think in terms of "if . . . then." For example:

- If you find you like listening to jazz . . . then buy a CD; download an album from an artist you're curious about; go to a jazz club.
- If you like decorating . . . then subscribe to a home décor magazine; decide to redo the bathroom à la Philippe Starck; take an interior design class.
- If you want to see what all this rock-climbing fuss is about . . . then find a nearby gym with a climbing wall; take an introductory lesson; join a club.

When you begin to nourish yourself with new challenges and experiences, the ones that fit you the best will naturally draw more of your attention, says Dr. Csikszentmihalyi. "If people pay attention to how they feel after doing something that requires skill and effort—and compare that to how they feel after watching TV for four hours—you should begin to realize the difference.

Hanley of the MsMindbody Web site compares the importance of investing in yourself to the classic advice you get from most financial experts to "pay yourself first." The wisdom there is that putting aside money for your savings and your security—even before you pay the bills—is the only way to make financial progress.

"It's a similar concept," says Hanley. "If you don't give to yourself first by enriching yourself, you'll become depleted. It's hard to wrap your brain around the fact that you are the most important person in the world to you—and that's okay!"

And if you're wondering whether investing in your health counts as a type of self-investment, that's in the next chapter.

6

Put Your Money Where Your Health Is

If I knew I was going to live this long,
I would have taken better care of myself.

—*Mickey Mantle*

I can honestly say that for most of my life I didn't put much effort into being healthy. The only time my health was a priority was when I spent a brief period living in Northern California. But when you live there, you really don't have a choice. If you're not drinking organic soy chai lattes and kayaking every weekend, you might as well shuffle back to Buffalo.

In fact, when I did move back East, I was shocked by how quickly the few health habits I'd acquired now deteriorated. Within a few months I was back to living a stressful, sedentary life, with zero outdoor activity and random encounters with the occasional fresh fruit or vegetable. My insomnia returned. My anxiety level went up. My skin didn't look so great. My energy was like a boat with a bad motor, surging then stalling. But as with humans everywhere, it didn't occur to me to improve ι Ͻοn the status quo until I had to—when I got pregnant.

At first I found most prenatal health advice to be so overwhelming in scope that it almost paralyzed me—so many Dos and Don'ts and Musts and Shouldn'ts and Don't Even Think about Its. But I had a baby on board now, and I had to be proactive. So rather than fret about whether I was meeting every last minuscule requirement, I decided the best route would be to focus on the bigger picture: simple, basic health maintenance. I might not live up to the standards of the pregnancy police, I reasoned, but if I could hit most of the recommended daily allowances, I'd be ahead of myself.

I bought a nine-month supply of vitamins and got some exercise each day, even if it was just a walk. I ate lots of protein and, yes, those green leafy vegetables nutrition experts are always waving at you. I learned to make fruit salad (to my amazement, it didn't take a PhD) and splurged on organic produce and fresh juices. If I was beat, I lay down for a rest or took a nap. I bought a yoga mat to do stretches at home. I spent more than I normally would have on seeing an acupuncturist every other week, and treated myself to various herbal teas for their supposed benefits. I hydrated, moisturized, and even invested in taking a meditation class—something I'd been meaning to try for years.

And I felt *great*. At first I thought it was a hormonal thing. As the trimesters passed, I began to realize that this wonderful, mellow feeling of capital H healthiness was more likely the result of taking truly excellent care of myself for the first time in . . . about four decades. I'm not discounting the benefits of pregnancy as well, but my total sense of well-being went beyond that: My moods were stable, my anxiety was low (one friend kept saying, "You're not wound up—are you okay?"), I was sleeping better than I had in years, I got one cold that winter instead of three—and I felt consistently, physically *good*.

I also felt like a sap. What would it have cost me to buy a few supplements, add some fresh produce to my diet, get out in the fresh air once a day, eat more protein, cut back on my vices, make time for unwinding—before I got pregnant? "What if you had been doing just these few basic things all along?" I asked myself. It was astonishing to think that for a rather minimal investment of money and time, I could have reaped the benefits of being tuned into my health years ago.

COMPOUNDING YOUR INVESTMENTS

It won't surprise you to know that rigorous scientific surveys have found a positive relationship between being healthy and feeling happy. (According to the quality-of-life survey by Glen Firebaugh at the University of Pittsburgh, only 5 percent of those in poor health say they're happy, compared to about half of those in excellent health.) But what you may find interesting is that being healthy and happy doesn't require turning into a tofu-eating, Pilates-obsessed, 3-percent-body-fat health nut. There's a kinder, gentler model that works just as well, scientists have found: Small but steady investments in just a slightly more healthy way of life yield big gains.

My favorite studies are those in which participants do a mild form of exercise once a week—like walking or gardening—and live to be one hundred. All right, that's a slight exaggeration, but one group of patients reduced their risk of dying of cardiac arrest by 70 percent, just by exercising once a week.

Another group cut their risk of heart disease and lowered their blood pressure significantly by investing in a mere three hours a week of moderate activity—that's seventeen minutes a day—as well as reducing their sodium intake and eating more fruits and vegetables.

> **Happiness consists of activity. It is a running stream, not a stagnant pond.**   —*Oliver Wendell Holmes*

Like my pregnancy experience, what these studies support is the physical equivalent of what financial investors call "dollar cost averaging," a strategy based on putting a steady amount of money into the market at regular intervals—which has the happy effect of minimizing your risk and maximizing your gains thanks to a minimal amount of effort. It's not as splashy as buying $10,000 worth of some hot new stock—but one thing that drives money advisers crazy is when would-be investors hesitate to put money into a retirement or investment account because they can contribute only small amounts. In fact, it's those little investments deposited over time that make a vast difference to your ultimate worth—and a similar principle applies to your health, said Dr. William Vollmer, a senior investigator with the Kaiser Permanente Center for Health Research, who was a coauthor on the heart disease study above. "These little preventive measures pay big dividends in the long run," he said.

"What this study showed is that people can make multiple lifestyle changes over the long term, and not only do these changes not have to cost you that much—it's only a little more expensive to eat fresh fruits and vegetables," Dr. Vollmer points out, "but these are things that are easily within our reach."

After all, some researchers have found that it's how healthy *you feel* that contributes most to your well-being, not how you measure up on an EKG. So although your physical well-being should be a core holding in your portfolio, your focus doesn't have to be on reaching some Olympic gold standard of health, but on doing what you can to make yourself feel good. Moreover, investing in your health has a comparable effect to putting money in the bank, according to Canadian economist John Helliwell. By assessing various factors, like job loss or illness, in terms of their income equivalents (a complex calculation designed to measure the economic impact of certain life events), Dr. Helliwell found that people view poor health as the equivalent of experiencing a financial loss of about $320,000.

Any way you slice it, most people know that feeling healthy is vital to their happiness, and that it's worth investing in. But the real reason that it should be a mainstay of your happiness portfolio is that being healthy pays double dividends: (1) There are few things in life more pleasurable than pure physical well-being, and (2) having that reservoir of good health gives you the wherewithal to get more from all the other areas of your life.

GOOD HEALTH LEADS TO
HAPPIER CHOICES

Elaine, fifty-seven, says she learned the value of investing in her own health about eight years ago, when she started working at an assisted-living facility in Peachtree City, Georgia. Although she wasn't in poor health at the time, she had the unusual experience of being able to observe dozens of people in their seventies, eighties, and nineties ("Our oldest is 104 right now," she says), all functioning at very different levels of well-being. "Some people are doing so well—they've kept their teeth, they're good eaters, they like to walk—and I wonder how they did that. How did they not get Alzheimer's or heart disease or osteoporosis?"

In getting to know people's case histories, Elaine says, she learned that although some people were blessed with good health all their lives, many had had a wake-up call and decided to make their health a lifelong priority. "Maybe they had breast cancer or some other devastating illness—but they beat it. In some cases that was thirty years ago, and now they're in their nineties."

Elaine realized she didn't need to wait for some illness to strike in order to change her habits. "When you start watching all these cool older people, you look at yourself in the mirror and think: Okay, how can I save what I have for as long as possible?"

At first Elaine's efforts were focused on basic health improvements. She cut back on sugar and avoided eating "those giant, American-size portions" at meals. As she started taking her own health sector more seriously, she began to put her money where her health was. She bought some good walking shoes and kept up her gym membership so she could hit the treadmill whenever possible. But because she loves the outdoors, she also makes a point of taking weekend trips so she can get to the beach or go hiking in the mountains. She took her twenty-two-year-old daughter and a friend to the Great Smoky Mountains recently, "and they ran to the top—while I thought I was going to die," she laughs. "You do get creakier as you get older."

Thanks to these small investments, not only did Elaine gradually find that her strength and stamina improved—and she lost a few pounds—she noticed that the quality of her life had gone up several notches. "I have more energy, I feel better, and I just enjoy life more," she says.

And her enjoyment didn't end there. The real payoff from investing in your health comes when you can turn around and get even more out of life. Feeling more upbeat than she had in a while, Elaine started spending more on hobbies like taking a pottery class, sewing, playing the piano, and bird watching—pastimes she used to love and always assumed she'd have the resources to pursue. "But the years go by, you get older and you think: When am I going to do these things I keep thinking I'll have time for?"

By investing a little more in her health, Elaine found she did have the time and money to enrich her life in these ways. And she knows the gains will keep coming. "I've seen what happens to people in their nineties. There's a big difference between those who decided to put their health first and the ones who didn't. That's the quality of life I want."

A FEEL-GOOD FORMULA

Note: Elaine's health regimen was based on doing things that felt good to her. The subjects in the heart disease study didn't have to run a triathlon; they found easygoing ways to exercise. So as you think about investing in your health, remember that this should be an exercise in pleasure, not discipline and deprivation. Unless you like that sort of thing. Whatever steps you take, make them fun, make them enjoyable. Economist John Helliwell points out that it's human nature to resist doing what's good for us. "The best way to make health-improving activities stick is to combine them with something else that has a life-satisfying kick."

For example, building in a social component is an excellent way to make sure your investment pans out, Dr. Helliwell says, pointing out that "people who suffer debilitating illnesses live longer when they are in a socially sustaining environment, with friends or loved ones." By the same token, you're more likely to keep up your jogging routine if you have a buddy to share it with, he says, or to stick with a sport if you find some friends, buy some equipment, and start a softball league.

> **Every patient carries her or his own doctor inside.**
>
> —*Albert Schweitzer*

Here are some ways to invest your money and time in your ongoing happy healthiness.

- **Pay a little more for really fresh or higher quality foods.** A coworker of mine would pay exorbitant amounts for top-notch olive oil, because she said it made everything she cooked taste better. Others pay extra for the benefits (and great taste) of organic products like grass-fed beef or poultry raised without questionable chemicals.
- **Give your gym membership a workout.** It's worth investing in a more deluxe gym—or shelling out for a membership with passport privileges—if it means you'll work out more regularly. Or join a gym that's close to your house, even if it costs more, because the more convenient it is, the more likely you are to go. Better for your health *and* your bottom line: According to one study of eight thousand gym members, about 80 percent weren't working out often enough to justify their membership fees—and were losing the equivalent of $700 a year.
- **Join a food co-op,** where you trade a small amount of time for access to fresher food at a lower price.
- **Sign up for a farm basket.** These are more common in rural areas, but some cities also have a service where you "subscribe" to a regular delivery of fresh produce. Search local listings.
- **Pay for personal care.** Many people today are tethered to health plans that limit their choice of physicians.

Sometimes it's a better investment to spend out of pocket to see a doctor whom you like and trust, and who spends time with you.

· **Splurge on delivery.** If you're more likely to cook nourishing meals if you don't have to shop, find out if your local supermarket delivers, or try an online grocer. With the time you save and the convenience you gain—never mind the nutritional boost—it's worth paying a small fee for such a big service.

· **Pay more for prewashed veggies.** True, the prewashed spinach and salads cost more, but if you're more likely to eat them when they're conveniently washed for you, it's a small price to pay to get all those B vitamins and fiber.

· **Invest in equipment you'll use.** Forget the rowing machine in the den if you're the outdoorsy type. A better buy for you is some sturdy footwear that will get you moving.

· **Explore alternative healing.** As the cost of traditional health care and prescription medicines rises, more people are investing in alternative therapies, including herbal supplements, teas, acupuncture, chiropractic, Reiki, and other modalities. According to a *New York Times* article, Americans spent about $27 billion on alternative health care, and 48 percent used at least one such remedy in 2004—many for basic well-being.

· **Enrich your brain.** One of the most potent ways to stave off mental deterioration and the onset of Alzheimer's is to exercise your mind. You can't join a mental gym, but

you can invest in a book of crossword puzzles or Su-
doku, stay connected to a social network, take classes
that keep you learning. As Elaine points out, these
things may sound like an investment for your golden
years, but they have a delightful side effect of enriching
your life now.

· **Pay for laughs.** Rent old Bugs Bunny cartoons, *All in the
Family* episodes, or whatever tickles your fancy. Buy a
collection of Dave Barry's books. Hit your local comedy
club. According to a study released in 2006 by the University of Maryland, laughter keeps your heart healthy
by dilating blood vessels and increasing blood flow.
Other studies have also found that laughter reduces
stress hormones, eases tension, and boosts the im-
mune system. Oh, and laughing makes you feel great. So
when you're planning a night out, spend a little more to
make sure you get your RDA of comedy.

· **Invest in bed.** Is there anything a good sex life can't
cure? Based on all the existing research, a satisfying sex
life can help you sleep better, protect against depression, boost your circulation, reduce the amount of stress
hormones in the body—and contribute to a happy relationship (which you'll see in chapter 9 is an investment
all its own). So if you're not sure whether to buy a new
DVD or perhaps something more sensual that might set
the mood, guess where you should put your money?

Above all, remember that financial concept of dollar cost averaging. Many of us justify our couch-potato leanings by say-

ing, "What difference will it make if I just sit here or go for a walk?" Well, now you know. You need to pick only one thing from the above list to start feeling better—and perhaps experience that upward spiral of well-being.

After all, investing in these health stocks will generate more happiness gains now—and maybe even a more financially secure and fulfilling future as well. According to 2006 estimates by Fidelity Investments, a couple who retires today is likely to spend $200,000 on health-related costs alone during a fifteen-to-twenty-year life span, thanks to rising prescription drug costs and Medicare premiums, plus other out-of-pocket expenses. By building a healthier life now, you could substantially reduce the financial hit you take as you age—and wouldn't that make you happy?

And speaking of money, it's time to move the discussion on to maximizing your financial health.

7

Pay Down Your Debt

I'm living so far beyond my income, we almost
may be said to be living apart.

—e.e. cummings

Until now we've been talking mainly about all the ways that getting caught up in today's consumer lifestyle will squash your quality of life. The other major problem with the getting-and-spending lifestyle is that, unchecked, it will wreak havoc with your financial stability. Specifically, I'm talking about getting into, living under, and not being able to get rid of—debt.

This isn't just a financial issue. Few things will make you more miserable than living under a constant cloud of financial strain. In a 2005 study conducted by Rutgers researcher Barbara O'Neill of over three thousand people in financial debt and distress, 42 percent said their health had been negatively affected by their money woes. Just over 58 percent of those specified that they suffered from stress, worry, tension, and anxiety, and nearly 20 percent said they'd experienced depression and insomnia as a result of being in financial straits.

According to a joint report, released in 2005 by academic scholars and business professionals, an estimated 30 million American workers—nearly one in four—are in a serious financial quandary, largely "from overuse of credit, as well as money and spending problems." Nearly half of those say their physical or mental well-being has been compromised as a result. E. Thomas Garman, professor emeritus at Virginia Tech University and one of the coauthors of the study, points out that problems arise when people overestimate how much borrowed money they can afford to live on. "It's the credit lifestyle," he says. "And when you're stretched financially, it causes anxiety—which adds another layer of tension to your life and carries over to your job, your home life, your relationship with your spouse and children."

Worse, those who get caught in debt's sticky web may find it harder to extricate themselves—not because it requires discipline or willpower, but because we live in such debt-friendly times. It's become comfortable to borrow, and people have become inured to living with levels of debt that would have been unthinkable just a decade or two ago. Robert Manning, author of *Credit Card Nation* and one of the leading authorities on debt in America, conducted a study with Lending Tree in 2005 that documents Americans' growing tolerance of debt at almost every stage of life.

"In the past people would have based their budget on 80% to 90% of their take-home pay," Dr. Manning says. "Now we see, based on the federal Survey of Consumer Finances, that people are living on close to 120% of their discretionary income." There are two reasons why being in debt cannot coexist with quality of life. The first has to do with the escalating level of tension and stress that debt brings, as I just mentioned; the second is simple arithmetic. Every dollar you spend servicing your debt is one less dollar you have to invest in the life you really want.

In other words, this is one line item you want off your balance sheet; having debt is like draining assets right out of your happiness portfolio.

WHEN DEBT TAKES YOUR LIFE AWAY

That was the position that Rebecca, thirty-seven, and Sean, thirty-one, found themselves in a few years ago. Although Rebecca was earning a good salary working for the United Nations, and Sean wasn't doing too badly as a freelance graphic designer, they were spending everything they earned—and quite a bit more. Their weakness: traveling. Rebecca's job often took her to exotic locations, "and we'd just tack on an extra week at the end of my business trips and make it a vacation," she says.

Like many people who overspend but are trying not to notice, their main rationale was that they were . . . saving! Rebecca's plane tickets were paid for by her job, so all they had to do was buy Sean a ticket and find some money for a hotel— and voilà! A cheap vacation. Except all those cheap vacations, plus eating out and other overspending habits, quickly added up to about $16,000 in debt.

Luckily, the couple was forced to face their debt problem because it had become a huge obstacle in taking their next step in life: relocating from the U.S. to Australia, where Rebecca was from. Debt maintenance was draining so much of their cash flow, they couldn't save any money toward their goal, which was making them miserable. "It was incredibly stressful to know that we were making good money—but a ridiculous amount of it was going toward our credit cards. Meanwhile, we had to keep postponing our move, which was the real dream we had."

> **Anybody who thinks money will make you happy hasn't got money.** —*David Geffen*

That's the true reason for anyone to get out of debt—you can't invest in your own happiness, your own dreams, when your money is feeding a plastic card.

When Rebecca and Sean realized the price they were paying—and that without drastic action to get out from under they'd never realize their dream of relocating Down Under—they put themselves in debt-payback boot camp. They cut back on travel, eating out, all unnecessary expenditures—even beer, which was hard for Sean—and made getting out of debt so they could save for Australia the priority.

"I don't know if we would have worked as hard without that goal," Rebecca admits. She used her knowledge of Excel to create pie charts, which showed their target savings—and their progress in paying off their debt. Every week she'd print out a new chart showing how much they'd saved and how much was going toward their credit cards—and she put them on the refrigerator. It took quite a bit of sacrifice, but within one year they'd saved $18,000—and by the time they moved to Australia, they'd paid off most of their debts.

"I still have about $2,500 left," Rebecca wrote in an e-mail from Australia, "because the move was a little more expensive than we imagined. But I'm still proud of how much we paid off— we can probably take care of the rest this year."

Getting out of debt, as it turned out, turned into an unexpected form of investment for Rebecca and Sean—an investment in a much richer way of life. Rebecca decided to go back to school to get her MBA—another investment she couldn't have afforded before. Sean decided he could afford to take up surfing. In getting out from under all that plastic, they rediscovered what it was like to live life. It wasn't just paying off the debt that did it, it was all the skills they mastered in order to gain control over their finances: knowing where their money went, learning to save, being able to set financial priorities.

LESS DEBT EQUALS MORE PEACE OF MIND

That's the secret bonus here. The awesome side effect that comes from getting a grip on debt is that it requires you to put your whole financial house in order.

Of course, debt is not always a result of financial irresponsibility. Divorce, unforeseen illness—life is full of unexpected and sometimes devastating expenses that can send even the most responsible folks spiraling into debt. For many, though, debt is a confluence of circumstances and bad habits, and breaking out of it requires straightening things up.

No matter the reason for your debt, the best way to beat the beast is a method I call Extreme Debt Reduction. It's not for the lazy, the hesitant, or those who want to get out of debt but don't really want to change their lifestyle. Sorry. This is only for folks who are serious about total debt elimination. This is a whole-life approach to draining all unnecessary debt from your life. Getting out of debt isn't just about being free of monthly bills, or saving thousands of dollars in interest—which it will—it's ultimately about feeling the power and the peace of mind of knowing that you're in control of your financial life.

There are many types of debt, but for now let's focus on credit card debt, which may be either the most common or the most demoralizing type of debt—or both. It's not that other types of debt are less important, but not all debt erodes your net worth. Your mortgage, student loans, and in some cases even home equity loans can be investments—in yourself or a property—that can yield substantial gains either in quality of life or in monetary profit.

So when you list all your debt, which you are about to do, put the worst debt first—because that's your payback priority—and "good" debt last, according to the list below. As you'll see, credit card debt is at the top of the list because next to owing money to a loan shark, that's the worst kind of debt. Back taxes are next (because those come with penalties and interest), and so on down the line to student loans and mortgages, which are certainly types of debt, but they're also considered investments. (A person who invests in a bachelor's degree, for example, is likely to earn nearly double the annual salary, on average, of someone who has only a high school diploma, according to the Census Bureau: about $45,000 versus $24,000.)

DEBTS BY PRIORITY:
- credit cards, store cards
- back taxes
- money borrowed from your 401(k)
- car loan(s)
- home equity loan or line of credit
- student loan
- small business loan
- mortgage

Some personal finance experts take a hard line about debt, and for them *all* debt is bad debt. Cash is king. I agree with that, to a degree, but some types of debt—like most credit cards and home equity loans and even back taxes—are so freighted with interest (and in some cases penalties and other fees) that your payments scarcely make a dent in what you owe. Mortgages are structured that way, too, in the sense that you pay off primarily just the interest you owe for the first several years. But during that time, ideally, your house may gain equity.

Many books have been written on the subject of debt alone, but I prefer those that emphasize a broader picture. What most people in debt need is a crash course in living more modestly, realigning their financial behavior so it reflects their values—

instead of a thousand impulse purchases and indulgences. Here are some titles to try:

- *The Millionaire Next Door*, by Thomas J. Stanley and William D. Danko
- *Money, a Memoir: Women, Emotions and Cash*, by Liz Perle
- *The Total Money Makeover: A Proven Plan for Financial Fitness*, by Dave Ramsey
- *Your Money or Your Life*, by Joe Dominguez and Vicki Robin
- *Deal with Your Debt: The Right Way to Manage Your Bills and Pay Off What You Owe*, by Liz Pulliam Weston

These are all excellent resources. I encourage you to consult them as well. The rest of this chapter is devoted to a single, laserlike method to blast the worst debt out of your life.

EXTREME DEBT REDUCTION IN FIVE STEPS

Nothing of what I'm about to tell you is new. Some of these steps will seem familiar. All of them are simple and direct. What's different about the Extreme Debt Reduction method is that if you take all the steps, in sequence, *with grit and determination*—they actually will get you out of debt. You don't have to do all five steps today. In fact, it's better if you distribute each of the tasks over a week or so. To that end I've included how long each step may take, so you can better fit it into your schedule. Ask any military strategist: Realistic planning is the key to success.

The other reality to bear in mind as you gear up to fight this particular opponent is that no battle is ever won without sacrifice. So ask yourself now: Are you ready to make some sacrifices? I'd love to tell you that you can enjoy your current lifestyle, add these few steps, and get out of debt. Unfortunately, your current lifestyle is probably what got you into debt. So the status quo has to go. This is boot camp. Just remember that the temporary discomfort you may experience is a small price to pay for honor, glory, and the financial peace of mind you'll feel when you're finally debt free.

> **The man who does not work for the love of work, but only for money, is not likely to make money nor find much fun in life.** —*Charles M. Schwab*

Step 1: Know the Enemy

The first step is to get busy and figure out exactly how much debt you have because: a) nobody really wants to know, and b) until you know, you won't know what you're up against—or what it will take for you to gain the upper hand.

To that end you will need:

- copies of all your current credit card bills and statements

- a calculator
- a folder

Write down exactly how much debt you have, to the penny, with which banks or institutions, at what interest rates. If you don't know or can't read all that fine print (and I sympathize; they use small type to keep us all clueless and confused), CALL THE COMPANY. That's why the toll-free number is there.

Please note that I have not included a handy worksheet here, as many books do. Who is going to write down what they owe in a book that anyone else could pick up and read? I want you to be honest and thorough. So after you write all this down, store your papers in your private Extreme Debt Reduction folder.

THIS STEP TAKES APPROXIMATELY
15 TO 30 MINUTES.

Step 2: Survey the Terrain

Use a free online debt calculator at any of the following Web sites to determine how long it will take you to pay down your debt, *given your current monthly payments.* Search on the following sites for "debt calculator"; I've found these to be the most reliable and easy-to-use:

- www.bankrate.com
- www.fool.com
- www.msn.com
- www.kiplinger.com

By using a debt calculator, you can figure out how quickly your current payment rate will make you debt free. For example: If you have a balance of $4,350 at 9% interest, and you're paying $100 a month (which is close to what the standard 2% minimum payment would be), it will take you 53 months to pay down your debt—assuming you never charge another penny of debt on that card, never make a late payment, never miss a payment. Write down how long you will be in debt, at your current rate of payment.

THIS STEP TAKES 10 TO 15 MINUTES.

Step 3: Explore Your Options

Now, using the same online calculator, plug in different payment amounts to see how much more quickly a higher payment will get you out of debt. (Using the same example above, if you upped your monthly payment to $150, you'd be debt free in about thirty-three months.)

Next plug in different deadlines. If you wanted to be debt free in two years, your monthly payments would be about $200. Escaping from debt within 12 months would require a payment of $380 per month. What seems possible now? Could you muster up $380 a month to be debt free *in a year*?

THIS STEP TAKES ABOUT 10 MINUTES.

Step 4: Choose Your Weapons

Now that you've weighed various options—different monthly payment amounts, various debt-free deadlines—you need to choose, based on your resources and the strength of your desire, what payment plan and time frame are ideal for you.

Keep your goal in mind and be as ruthless as you can. Not just because it's fun to think like an antidebt warrior, but because the credit card deck is stacked against you and me and anyone else who is carrying a balance. For example, you won't get anywhere paying just the minimum payment. They should call that the stay-in-debt payment, because that's what it is. Even the standard advice from many personal finance experts is inadequate: People say you should pay at least double your minimum payment. Given that the minimum payment is between 2% and 4% of the balance, doubling it could mean (depending on your interest rate) that you're paying only a little more than the interest you're accruing and a crumb of the principal.

To make real progress, I suggest making your minimum payments *quadruple* what your card's so-called minimum is.

Next: Don't leave it to your all-too-human self to stick to this plan. Set up automatic payments from your bank account to your credit card. You can set this up online, at your bank's Web site. If you aren't sure whether the institution offers automatic payments or transfers, call them. Usually this service is free and takes only a few minutes to set up. And these days most online transactions are safe and secure. Consider making weekly payments, which reduces principal and interest more rapidly.

COMPLETING THIS STEP COULD TAKE 15 MINUTES OR A FEW
HOURS AS YOU WEIGH YOUR BUDGET AND POSSIBLY CONSULT
WITH YOUR SPOUSE. MEANWHILE, READ STEP 5.

Step 5: Attack

If you're like most people, the logic of paying more so you can get out of debt faster will seem irresistible—except for one thing. Where do you get the extra money?

That's easy: How gutsy and creative are you willing to be? It's true that even a small payment increase will help, and if that's the limit of your resources right now, do that. But if you want to obliterate your debt, you have to throw significantly larger chunks of money at it. But not forever! This battle may be fierce, but the whole point of Extreme Debt Reduction is to get it over with fast—*so you can invest more in your life.*

KNOWING WHERE YOUR MONEY GOES

The object, while you're in Extreme Debt Reduction mode, is to divert as much cash as you can from unimportant expenditures and devote it to obliterating debt. Before you commit to a plan of attack, I'd like you to review the spending exercises from chapters 2 and 3. If you didn't get to these yet, it's imperative that you do so now. Debt is a problem of "spending more than you have," so you can't make any progress on your debt until you have a grip on your spending.

A close examination of your spending habits often yields more cash, but in order to aggressively attack your debt, here are some other ways you can earn or obtain more money. Many of these measures may seem uncomfortable—and they are. But again, they're temporary.

- **Stop the spending reflex.** For people in debt, it's not just that you have to spend less, *you have to stop spending*. Leave your credit cards home so you're not tempted to buy things you don't have cash for, and so you can break the plastic addiction. Before you buy as much as a pack of gum, learn to ask yourself whether each purchase is necessary. It may take a while to acquire these new habits. But soon you'll realize how much of your spending was superfluous.

- **Move in with family or friends.** Even if you're an adult. Even if you have children. Plenty of people take a short, not-always-depressing sabbatical from their independent lives and move in with relatives or friends to save money. Set a fixed time period; move out when you say you will; discuss all arrangements (money, chores, groceries, privacy) up front and keep the dialogue open so that resentment doesn't build.

- **Get a roommate.** If you have a spare room, or can create one that's rentable, this is an excellent way to generate cash. Same caveats as above.

> **Learn to cook! That's the way to save money.**
> —*Julia Child in* Julia Child's Kitchen *(1975)*

- **Work more.** If your time is already tapped out, this may not be an option, but if you have the stamina for even a part-time weekend job, every little bit counts. Put those paychecks directly toward paying off debt; don't let that money see the inside of your checking account for even a minute.

· **Borrow.** If you have a friend, coworker, or relative who can loan you some cash, interest-free—so you can pay off some or all of your debt—this could significantly reduce the total amount you repay. Again: Set clear terms regarding the length of the loan and what your repayment plan is and stick to 'em.

· **Sell assets.** When Lynnette Khalfani, author of *Zero Debt*, found herself $100,000 in the hole thanks to massive spending on credit cards, she did everything she could to pay it off, including selling a chunk of land she'd invested in. If you don't have a major asset, sell whatever you can part with on eBay, Craigslist.com, or even a humble yard sale. You never know when those bald eagle salt 'n' pepper shakers you got for your wedding will bring in a tidy sum.

· **Start saving.** It may sound counterintuitive, but in order to be debt free, you have to build up enough savings to cover those unexpected expenses—so that you don't fall into debt again. If you're using the 60% Solution from chapter 3, aim to save 10 percent of your income per month, but even if you set aside only ten dollars a week in a savings account that's not attached to an ATM card (very important!) or transferable to your checking account, that money acts as insurance against further debt. That way when you need new tires or your winter heating bill is super-high, you have a cushion of cash you can lean on instead of plastic.

· **Don't touch that nest egg.** As tempting as it might be to tap your retirement savings, in most cases, withdrawing that money comes at a heavy price in terms of paying both taxes and penalties on what you withdraw. Withdrawing $5,000 from a traditional IRA, for example, would be subject to $1,400 in taxes (assuming a 28% income tax rate) plus a 10 percent penalty of $500. Suddenly you get only about $3,100 in cash. While there are exceptions (www.fool.com has an excellent section on the ins and outs of IRAs), none of them apply to paying off your credit cards or other debts.

· **Put all bonuses, refunds, birthday money, rebates, and any other windfalls toward debt.** All of them. Enjoy the no-frills, few-treats lifestyle for a little while and let that shrinking balance be your reward.

*THIS STEP REQUIRES THAT YOU MAKE SOME CHOICES
AND COMMIT TO THEM—WHICH MIGHT TAKE A WHILE.
EITHER WAY, YOU WILL NEED THAT EXTRA PACKAGE OF
GRIT AND DETERMINATION.*

Rather go to Bed supperless than rise in Debt.
> —*Ben Franklin*, Poor Richard's Almanack

Now that you've reviewed the five steps, your brain is probably humming with possibilities. By analyzing how much debt you have and weighing how quickly you can pay it off—as well as

brainstorming ways to generate fatter payments—you're getting into Extreme Debt Reduction mode. Great!

The beauty of this system is that once you get going, it's self-
reinforcing. You might think you'll miss the free-spending
lifestyle, but you're going to love being able to invest in the rest
of your happiness portfolio even more—particularly being able
to use your money to buy yourself greater peace of mind, as
you'll see in the next chapter.

8

Buy Yourself
Peace of Mind

I'm fixing a hole where the rain gets in
And stops my mind from wandering . . .

—Lennon & McCartney

It's sad that people often think of money as a source of stress, because if you read the original instructions, it was designed to alleviate all kinds of angst and woes. In fact, stress relief can be one of your money's most important functions, if you remember to use it that way. Thus a small but vital sector in your portfolio should be an assortment of small investments devoted to increasing your peace of mind whenever and wherever possible. By that I mean:

- Investing in greater security or safety
- Shelling out more for convenience
- Paying for expertise
- Investing in simpler solutions

· Spending money to fix what you keep putting off
· Forgoing false economy in order to enjoy a greater quality of life overall.

These may not sound like direct investments in happiness per se, but they are. By using your money to extinguish all the piddly little brushfires that cause you to worry and fret—or dousing as many as you can—you gain priceless serenity. At times these expenditures may seem like extravagances. And maybe sometimes they are. But quite often the emotional return on this particular form of investment is so high that it's more than worth whatever the mere financial cost might be.

Unlike investing in your health or buying back your time or some of the other topics we've covered, peace of mind is harder to describe in general terms. Far more powerful are specific examples from the lives of real people who have tried to tackle a problem from several angles—and finally just used that magic bullet, cash, to put an end to their difficulty. My husband calls this "The willingness to say: To hell with it!" (Actually, he used more colorful language, but you get the idea.)

Many of us suffer from wishful thinking when it comes to coping with life's loose ends. You tell yourself you will fix that dripping faucet or review your 401(k) holdings or clean out that closet—it's not nuclear physics, is it?—but six or twelve or eighteen months later, nothing has changed. The result is a slow buildup of stress that's the psychic equivalent of plaque clogging your arteries—and it's unnecessary, because in many cases a simple financial investment would have solved the problem and prevented all that angst.

Quite often we tell ourselves we don't have the money to fix a certain problem. And while sometimes the money is lacking, what I see far more often is that people just don't want to spend money coping with what seems like a tedious, mundane little problem that should just go away on its own. But it doesn't.

I knew a woman who bought a new home and was afraid to cook anything on her stove because the burners didn't light properly. She lived without a working stove for over six months—but not because she was broke. She had the money to fix it. She just didn't want to make a simple investment to eliminate the stress and inconvenience she was enduring. Meanwhile, a relatively inexpensive repair job would have solved the problem, restored her kitchen to its full working capacity, and eliminated the merry-go-round of takeout meals and microwave dinners she had been juggling.

My husband and I learned this lesson when we decided to repair the sagging gutter above the front porch on our house. By ourselves. We bought the new gutter, the whatchamacallits that you use to screw on the gutter, and probably some tar or something. We had no idea what we were doing, but we were determined to fix this problem on our own. Of course, fear and cluelessness soon clouded our good intentions—and we stalled. And the gutter continued to overflow, causing further damage to the stone wall below . . . so now we had two things to worry about (which is always the way, isn't it?). The situation festered this way for, oh, about a year. Weekends would come and go. "Hon, we really should fix the gutters," one of us would say. "Yeah, totally, we should," the other would agree. Then we'd ignore it some more. Until finally the stress wore us down and we surrendered to the fact that this was a job for a pro. And we hired one.

Then we got the pleasure of kicking ourselves for many weeks afterward, once we realized that the relief of solving this problem was worth ten times the money—about $800—we'd spent taking care of it.

So the cost-benefit moral of my story is: You may not be able to throw money at all your problems, but a few relatively small investments can go a long way toward restoring your sanity—and freeing up your valuable time and energy for pursuits that are much more rewarding. You know what keeps you up at night better than I do, so consider the following list as fuel for some creative thoughts about how you might spend extra to make your life as pleasant and stress-free as possible.

- **Pay for an upgrade.** If your clunky old computer won't cut it anymore (and you don't want to spend big bucks on a new one), pay a tech expert—or savvy college kid—to upgrade your system so you can roam the Web at will, run more sophisticated programs, and make the most of what technology can do for you.
- **Accommodate yourself.** When Fran and Mike travel to see their daughter, they've decided that it's worth spending money for the convenience and comfort of staying at a nearby motel rather than roughing it on her lumpy futon. "She may have just graduated from college, but we're used to our creature comforts," Fran says. "This makes for a happier visit for everyone."

- **Hire some help.** At forty-one, Jon, a photographer in San Francisco, finally decided to join a gym in order to take off the weight he gained when he quit smoking. But rather than drive himself crazy trying to figure out the machines, he paid $200 for five sessions with a trainer. "I didn't want to mess around, I just wanted to lose the weight," he says, "and it was worth paying someone to tell me what to do so I could get moving and get the results I wanted."

- **Pay for productivity.** Like many new moms, Karen, a teacher in Ann Arbor, was suffering from a backlog of unpaid bills and other chores that she and her partner couldn't seem to get on top of in the months after their son was born. Although they couldn't afford even part-time child care at that point, Karen came up with a compromise—and hired a babysitter for a couple of hours each week so they could tackle all the various headaches that were building up around the house. "That turned out to be one of the best things I'd ever done for my sanity," she says.

- **Dig yourself out of a hole.** Not everyone who has a garden gets a green thumb to go with it—a fact I've had to face myself. So why struggle with weeds and seeds, and whether it's time to plant the bulbs or prune the geraniums, when you can buy a ready-made kit that provides a blueprint for your garden for as little as $24.95? Do an Internet search for "preplanned gardens," or go to www.bluestoneperennials.com or www.directgardening.com to check out their selection.

- **Invest in a money manager.** This being a book about money, I'd be remiss if I didn't recommend one of the most direct ways to build peace of mind, and that's hiring a qualified adviser to develop a plan for how best to manage your money over the long term. Whether you pay someone a flat fee or by the hour, this can seem like an expensive choice—ranging from a few hundred to a few thousand dollars—but imagine the relief and satisfaction of knowing that you have a financial strategy leading you toward your goals! I offer specific resources about finding a financial planner in the next chapter.

- **Take it easy.** Given how quickly a few frazzled moments can add up to a bad week, this is one of my top ways to invest in peace of mind: Use money to purchase some much-needed convenience. Here is one example: When choosing between the bus, which costs $15 and gets you to the airport in 45 minutes, versus a car service, which costs $35 and will take 25 minutes, consider your sanity as well as your wallet. Or: If you know that wrapping, weighing, and getting to the post office to send holiday gifts will take you until January—pay a little extra for the store or Web site's delivery charge. If it will ease your mind and it's a choice that won't break the bank, I say spend the money.

> **Money frees you from doing things you dislike. Since I dislike doing nearly everything, money is handy.**
>
> —*Groucho Marx*

BUY YOURSELF THE RIGHT STUFF

There's another way that we cheat ourselves out of peace of mind, and that's by giving in to false economy: Buying things on the cheap in order to save—only to end up spending just as much or more to replace the low-quality item you bought in the first place. Or: refusing to spend a little more on enjoying life on the grounds that "it costs too much." Shouldn't the better things in life cost a little more?

I learned this lesson, believe it or not, with regard to vacuum cleaners. From the time I rented my first apartment after college to the day I moved in with my husband—a span of about fifteen years—I relied on a mix of secondhand vacuum cleaners and cheap Dustbuster-type things that needed constant replacing. So for years I found vacuuming, not fun to begin with, a particularly onerous chore. Then one day I got fed up and spent $250 on the cheapest version of the most high-end vacuum cleaner I could find: a Miele. It was like graduating from your sister's beat-up VW Rabbit to a Maserati. This thing was a model of aerodynamic dirt-sucking perfection. It was so well-designed, in terms of movement and flexibility, vacuuming became something close to fun. Five years later it still runs like a Swiss watch, and I can't believe how much this one slightly pricey investment has added to my quality of life.

> **A wise man should have money in his head, but not his heart.** *—Jonathan Swift*

Sadly, breaking the habit of false economy can be hard because it's usually practiced in the name of financial sanity, or simply saving money, even though you rarely save anything (as I can tell you based on the small fortune I spent on Dustbusters). Take gas—most people look for the cheapest gas prices they can find. In fact, your car may last longer if you occasionally spend more for the more expensive grade. What's a better investment—saving a few dollars at the pump, or spending those extra dollars in order to save thousands on buying a whole new car before it's time?

The bottom line is that false economy is a poor investment, financially and emotionally. In the end you rarely save money—often you spend more—and you inevitably add to your daily hassle or compromise your quality of life. Here are some ways you might be committing false economy in your own life:

- **The bargain that isn't.** You buy sponges and dishwashing liquid at the dollar store—but what you buy is of such poor quality that the sponges go to pieces, and it takes twice as much dish soap to clean anything, so that you're back at the dollar store a week later. Lather, rinse, repeat until you get tired of watching your money go down the drain.
- **Skimping on pleasure.** An old and dear friend is in town and wants to go out to dinner. You'd rather not waste money on a big night out, so you meet your friend, but order only a cup of soup, and then spend all night fretting about how much the tip will be and whether your friend thinks you're a loser—instead of shelling

out a few extra bucks to relax, enjoy a full meal, and have a great time with your pal that isn't freighted with all that unnecessary worry.

· **Throwing good money after bad.** You buy the two-for-$20 shoes at the discount store—and have to throw them away in three months when they wear out, and then buy new shoes again. What if you spent $60 for one pair of shoes that would last you a year? It would be cheaper than spending $20 every three months—and less to worry about (and better for the environment).

· **The price of martyrdom.** You want to attend a friend's weekend wedding. Should you spend eight exhausting hours driving (plus the gas and wear and tear on your car)—or should you pay perhaps twice as much as the drive would cost for a two-hour plane ride and the plea-sure of a much more fun and easygoing weekend?

· **Doing without.** For three years after their marriage, Dan and Petra, both film editors in New York, lived with a mismatched set of dining room chairs—a hodgepodge from his old life and hers, none in very good condi-tion—and the sheer discomfort of having to look at them, never mind sit on them, "was like sleeping on gravel," Petra says. They didn't buy new chairs, or even a nicer set of used chairs, because they were upgrading other things—and they fed themselves the classic line: "We can't afford it right now." But if they had known how much happier they'd be, how much more pleasant each and every meal would be once they were sitting on comfortable chairs, "I would have spent the money years earlier," Dan says. (Especially since they ended up buying them at IKEA for half of what they thought they would have to spend.)

Next, I discuss the importance of investing in the greatest source of peace of mind: saving for a secure future.

9

Invest in Security

Put not your trust in money,
but put your money in trust.

—*Oliver Wendell Holmes*

The giant question mark of retirement keeps a lot of people up at night—and no wonder. How are you supposed to create a game plan that will get you through the Utterly Unknowable Unknowns of the future?

You know you're supposed to be saving—but even the most prudent savers can only "guesstimate" what their lives will look like, what will constitute enough to live on in twenty, thirty, forty years. To make matters more complicated, even as I type, the whole picture of retirement is being painted over. Pensions are vanishing; Social Security is shrinking to the size of a little Godiva chocolate. Yet people are living longer, and for many the notion of retiring to a quiet hammock somewhere has lost its allure, largely because many of today's retirees either want to—or will have to—keep working.

At the risk of repeating bad news you've already heard: According to the Center for Retirement Research at Boston College (CRR), the majority of Americans are way behind on their savings: More than one out of every four employees do not contribute to their company's 401(k) plan (one in three by some studies). And even then, a mind-boggling 55 percent of employees cash out those savings when they switch jobs. Based on current savings trends, or the lack thereof, some retirement models indicate that as median-wage workers near retirement, many will have saved less than $50,000.

Given these numbers, it seems that many people must be counting on Social Security to provide a safety net when they retire. But I pray you are not one of them. According to the CRR, the average Social Security allotment today replaces only about 42 percent of preretirement income—and it will soon cover even less, as new Medicare and tax provisions take effect. *Yet over a third of retirees depend on Social Security for 90 percent or more of their incomes in retirement.*

INVESTING IN RETIREMENT

As you can imagine, millions of Americans suffer chronic anxiety about the future for all these reasons, but largely because they worry about not having enough money to live on when they retire. Not surprisingly, the people who report being happiest in their retirement are those with the steadiest income, according to a brief by the CRR.

How can you alleviate your own anxieties about the future—and free yourself to relax and enjoy the present? Do the one thing everyone is afraid to do: Start planning. According to a study by American Express of about 1,400 people ages 40 to 64, those who sought help from a financial planner were far less anxious about retirement than those who hadn't (and they'd saved about twice as much money). That doesn't mean you should dash out and hire a financial pro this minute; rather it speaks to the importance of taking control of these issues, which is what this chapter is all about.

Unlike the other core holdings in your happiness portfolio, investing in retirement takes place on two levels: investing the time and energy it requires for you to take the reins of your financial future—and then learning to use your money more wisely now so that you can secure that future.

The good news is that it's not that hard. Really. You'll be amazed by how much relief you'll feel just by facing a few realities and running some numbers now—not to mention the great, big exhale these simple steps will bring you down the line. So let's get started.

Don't worry, I'm not going to bore you with a long sermon on the advantages of triple tax-free bonds or how to bequeath an annuity. I have only one chapter here, and the field of retirement planning has already filled countless volumes and many Web sites. Think of this as the pregame show. I'm going to give you the lowdown on some basic principles and provide the information you need to take the following essential steps:

- Develop a clearer vision of what your retirement lifestyle will look like.
- Calculate a ballpark figure for what that will cost.
- Choose simple but profitable ways to invest now.
- Understand what some of the key financial issues are in planning for the future so you can ask the right questions while moving forward.
- Relax and enjoy a greater happiness dividend now, knowing that you've taken control of your money and your life.

ORIENTATION: YOU ARE HERE

What most people want to know when they think about retirement is: How much? Am I saving enough? How much is enough? How big does my nest egg need to be? Half a million dollars? Three million dollars?

Naturally these questions are so daunting that the human tendency is to put your head in the sand and cross all your fingers—this is the magic way to make things turn out all right. In reality that's where things go terribly wrong.

According to an economic theory called "hyperbolic discounting," one of the reasons people don't save for the future isn't that we're scared, lazy, or clueless (although sometimes that's also the case), it's because most people have a tendency to value what they have in the present—and discount what they *may* have in the future. Thus spending cash today is easier than saving it for some hazy day when you're seventy-seven and may need that money to live on.

> **You can't expect to hit the jackpot if you don't put a few nickels in the machine.** —*Flip Wilson*

So what's the solution to that basic human reluctance to look ahead? As we all know, there are a blizzard of unknowns, but I believe that leaving the future as an empty fog only increases anxiety—and that destructive I'll-deal-with-this-later attitude. If economists are right, and people tend to discount the future, there's no better way to combat that inertia than first to envision what sort of life you'd like to lead when you're no longer technically young.

You may be too far away from retirement age to have any idea of what "the rest of your life" might look like. Or you might have conflicting visions: You may want to retire somewhere warm and raise prize begonias—or stay where you are, near family and friends, and work part-time. Or watch *Jeopardy* and volunteer. You may not have saved two nickels. You may have saved a million bucks. So can we answer every question here? No.

But you don't need to answer every question right now: You and I and most people need the security and serenity of knowing that we have a broad-based plan and a sense of control over that plan, which will evolve over time. So let's borrow a phrase from the well-known Buddhist author Pema Chodron, and make "Start where you are" the mantra for this chapter, to which I would add: "And plan based on what you can see from here."

EXERCISE
Your Life in Pictures

If you already know or have a pretty good inkling about what you'd like your later years to be, write it down here. Don't worry if you don't have a clear picture—because I haven't a clue myself, and plenty of people aren't sure, either. For now, all you need is a basic outline.

If you know your vision, please describe it here:

_____

_____

_____

_____

_____

_____

If you aren't sure, please check off any of the following statements that apply to you now (don't worry that they may change in the future). *When I retire, I'd like to:*

☐ Have paid off my mortgage and other debts.

☐ Sell my house and move to a small, manageable apartment.

☐ Move to a cute little college town and take classes.

☐ Buy a boat and spend half the year sailing.

☐ Not have any money worries.

☐ Not work.

☐ Start my own business.

☐ Be in excellent health.

☐ Move near my children and help raise my grandkids.

☐ Get another degree.

☐ Keep working or consulting in my current field.

☐ Work or consult in another field. (If you know what that might be, write that down here: _____

_____.)

☐ Do something creative like paint or write a book/screen-play.

☐ Devote most of my time to my favorite hobby,

_____.

☐ Nothing in particular, just enjoy a relaxing life.

As you look over the items you've checked off, take note of the price tags that may or may not be attached to those visions. Note your desires and priorities. You aren't wedded to anything—unless, by chance, you're planning to retire very soon. And unless you're extremely lucky and know exactly how you'd like to spend your later years, it could take a while for this vision to unfold. That's fine. Be patient. This exercise will help you connect your present financial situation to your long-term life plan. So even if turning sixty or seventy seems far away, remember the mantra *Start where you are, and plan based on what you can see from here.* Even if all you know is that you'd like to have your mortgage paid off so you can quit work and enjoy a relaxing life, that alone can influence many financial decisions now. For example:

- You might need to accelerate your payments in order to pay off your mortgage by retirement age.
- You might want to invest in regular home repairs now, so you don't have to pay for them when you're older.
- Then you can either live in your home with very low expenses, or sell it and move to a retirement community or an apartment.
- Unless you'll be happy literally doing nothing—nada, zip!—you might want to consider whether "nothing" means having a nice garden, a very large TV, your own fishing boat, or being able to fly across the country to visit loved ones. And how might you afford those things?

FINANCIAL DECISIONS NOW AFFECT THE FUTURE

How are you supposed to calculate what your projected lifestyle will cost?

Consider this: Most retirement plans are based on the idea that you'll be living on about 80 percent of your current income. That means, whatever lifestyle you can afford now is about what you'll be able to afford in the future—for one simple reason: Your savings rate is determined by your present income. It's really hard to save for a lifestyle that's much better than the one you're living now. It's not impossible, and certainly in retirement your money will be directed toward different things—you won't need to maintain a family-size abode; you may be done paying for college; you may not need to maintain a work wardrobe; you may not even need a car, depending on where you live—so your savings may go further. But it's best to keep the cost of your current lifestyle in mind as a benchmark.

> **I have enough money to last me the rest of my life, unless I buy something.** —*Jackie Mason*

It's also an important reality check for those of you who have more deluxe ideas about what your quality of life should look like in your golden years. Since most calculations about how much to save are based on your current standard of living (including the method we'll use in a moment), you may want to measure your retirement dreams against what you can afford now. If you live a quiet life in Minneapolis and hope to retire to a quiet life in Florida, saving based on your current income probably will get you there. If you plan to buy a fishing boat and move to St. Lucia, well, you probably need to save more aggressively.

Don't let the particulars (or the lack of them) make you throw up your hands. Remember: This is the pregame show! The real goal at this stage is to develop enough of a strategy that you begin to make more conscious financial decisions about the future—so that you can relax and enjoy your life even more now.

Seattle-based financial adviser Bill Schultheis is the author of *The Coffeehouse Investor*, a smart little book about how to invest without stress. Schultheis points out that most of us, particularly when we're young, like to think retirement will happen . . . one day. "So most of the time we make various financial decisions, assuming that retirement is far off," he says. In reality, what you do now financially has a powerful effect on your quality of life down the line. If you saved an extra $100 a month now in a tax-deferred account, for example, that could amount to an extra $113,000 in thirty years when you retire.

Could you save an extra $25 a week if you knew it would grow into a tidy little sum like that? As you can see, those extra lattes, expensive shoes, a new case for your iPod, take on a new significance—and they should. The $3 you spend on a cappuccino today is worth approximately $65 in a few decades. That's what's known as the time value of money, and it's something you'll be giving a lot more thought to as we move forward.

A REAL COUPLE LOOKS AHEAD

Now let's look at a real-life couple and what their retirement plans are. Although I had to change their names, all the other details, including the numbers, are real. In this section I also provide the simple formula, in the form of a worksheet, that I used to calculate the amount this couple would need as a retirement nest egg.

Terri and Mark live in Ohio, with their three-year-old daughter, Jo. Terri is forty and Mark is thirty-eight; they hope to retire in about thirty years. Their combined income now is about $70,000 a year. They have a little more than that socked away in 401(k)s and other tax-deferred accounts. Luckily, Mark's parents have set aside a college-savings plan for little Jo, so although Terri would like to save more to supplement those funds (for Jo's books and other school expenses), they can probably afford to focus on their own future for now.

In fact, one of the most-often-ignored pieces of financial advice is that you should, indeed, save for your own retirement first. If you have the luxury to simultaneously fund your future and your children's education—go for it. But it's far more prudent to make sure your future is secure as your children head to college and beyond because (1) they can rely on you as a secure base, if needed, and (2) your financial problems won't become theirs.

To figure out what sort of a nest egg Terri and Mark will need in thirty years, I used the following worksheet, and you can, too. Why choose this one out of the bazillion other retirement worksheets and calculators available? Because it's simple enough to give you a decent rough estimate for your target nest egg as well as how much you should be saving per month to meet that goal—in about ten minutes or less.

RETIREMENT PLANNING FUNDAMENTALS

If you're new to retirement calculations, please take a moment to digest a few of the basic guidelines of this process:

1. Retirement calculators and worksheets like this one are based on a variety of factors, including your age, your target retirement date, how much you have saved, what those investments are likely to earn, how much Social Security you might receive, what other investments you

might have (like real estate) or windfalls you might get (like an inheritance), and how long you're likely to live. This worksheet uses fewer variables, so you can adjust the final figures according to your own specifics.

2. There are certain assumptions about retirement planning that most calculations are based on:

    • Ideally, you should save a nest egg large enough so you can live on the interest it generates.

    • Every year you should withdraw no more than 4 percent of your assets to live on, in theory leaving the principal untouched.

    • You'll need only 70 to 80 percent of your current income in retirement, because you'll be spending less on taxes, housing, clothes, commuting, and consumption in general. (You also won't be saving for retirement.)

    • You'll be getting a small Social Security stipend.

3. There's quite a bit of gray area in those assumptions.

    • You don't know how long you're going to live, or whether your savings will have to last for thirty years or fifteen years.

    • You may need to calculate retirement based on closer to 100 percent of your current income if your living expenses aren't going to change very much. For example, you may be paying off a mortgage (60 percent of retirees today still are), or you might be working for a few more years (and paying taxes and commuting costs)—or both. The worksheet I use is based on retiring on 90 percent of your current income.

- What you get in Social Security may be negligible and you may want to discount those benefits entirely (many financial planners suggest planning for your retirement as though Social Security won't exist; then if it does, it's gravy!).
- Last, you may plow through your entire nest egg and *Die Broke*, as the title of one book has it—because you can't afford to live on interest alone, as the standard models would have you do.

CAVEATS ABOUT YOUR CALCULATIONS

I'm explaining all this because most of these formulas attempt to provide you with a fairly conservative estimate of the "ideal amount" you should save. For example, the notion of drawing down only 4 percent of your savings per year may sound very conservative—and that you'd end up leaving a lot of your money behind. Thing is, 4 percent is the amount that has been shown in countless calculations to make your nest egg last the longest—no matter what the stock market does, and to a degree no matter what the unexpected brings in your own life.

Also, this worksheet presumes that you'll retire at sixty-five, but you may not retire until later. In order to calculate the most basic, down-and-dirty amount, you have to give up on aaaaaaall those unknowns for the next five to ten minutes. You don't know what your investments will be worth by the time you retire. You don't know whether that house you'll buy ten years from now might yield you a windfall of $500,000. You don't know if you're going to be retiring in sickness or in health. But you have to move forward anyway.

> **How can I be secure? Through amassing wealth beyond all measure? No. And what's beyond all measure? That's a sickness. That's a trap. There is no measure.**
>
> —*Roma, in* Glengarry Glen Ross *by David Mamet*

You can use the worksheet included here, or you can go online and use one of the many retirement calculators there:

Kiplinger.com
Dinkytown.com
Choosetosave.org/ballpark
Money.com/tools
http://www.bloomberg.com/analysis/calculators
/retire.html
Several others are listed at: www.activeretirement.com.

Online calculators are pretty crude because most don't let you make adjustments based on your own situation; some assume a large Social Security supplement while others ask you to enter that number from your own Social Security statements; the results you get with one may differ wildly from those you get with another. Alas, this is an inexact science. For the most accurate analysis of your finances, you may want to hire a financial planner, an option I discuss below in the investment section.

8-STEP RETIREMENT WORKSHEET

Assume Retirement Age at 65	Terri & Mark income = $70,000	Your Numbers
1. Annual income needed at retirement in today's dollars *(multiply income by 90% or .90)*	$63,000	
2. Social Security benefits *(use 20% of current salary, up to 20K in annual benefits)*	$12,600	
3. Income needed in retirement *(Line 1 minus Line 2)*	$50,400	
4. Total nest egg needed by retirement, in today's dollars *(Line 3 times 20)*	$1.08 million	
5. Amount already saved for retirement	$71,000	
6. Value of savings at retirement, in today's dollars *(Line 5 times investment growth factor; see next chart)*	$181,760	
7. Savings still needed in today's dollars *(Line 4 minus Line 6)*	$826,240	

(continued)

ASSUME RETIREMENT AGE AT 65	TERRI & MARK INCOME = $70,000	YOUR NUMBERS
8. Monthly amount they need to save	$1,735	
(Line 7 times monthly savings factor; see next chart)		

This chart assumes 7 percent growth, 3 percent inflation, and investment in tax-deferred account.

RETIREMENT WORKSHEET FACTORS

YOUR AGE	INVESTMENT GROWTH FACTOR	MONTHLY SAVINGS FACTOR
21	5.62	0.0007
23	5.19	0.0008
25	4.80	0.0009
27	4.44	0.0010
29	4.10	0.0011
31	3.79	0.0012
33	3.51	0.0013
35	3.24	0.0015
37	3.00	0.0017
39	2.77	0.0019
41	2.56	0.0021
43	2.37	0.0024

45	2.19	0.0028
47	2.03	0.0032
49	1.87	0.0038
51	1.73	0.0046
53	1.60	0.0055
55	1.48	0.0069
57	1.37	0.0090
59	1.27	0.0126
61	1.17	0.0196
63	1.08	0.0408

That may sound like a daunting amount Mark and Terri need to save—and certainly they thought so when I told them. But whatever your target savings amount turns out to be, when you do this calculation yourself, don't freak out. Some of us are on target financially, some aren't. Maybe you can't ramp up your savings this year, but next year you can. The point is that you'll make the necessary adjustments in your financial life today only if you keep that bull's-eye amount front-of-mind.

Here are some other facts to weigh:

1. Like most calculations, this one assumes that you won't be touching your nest egg when you retire, because you'll be living off the interest. *But your nest egg can be less if you plan to live on part of your savings.* It's not conventional wisdom, but it's what Terri and Mark and many other people plan to do. In order to make sure they have a decent standard of living when they retire, they will draw down some of their savings—which

means their daughter will have a smaller inheritance, and they expose themselves to some additional risk. This is a sacrifice many people are willing to consider.

2. Many people will be earning some kind of income for a few years into their "retirement," which also may reduce the need for saving as much. For example, if Mark and Terri worked part-time for just five years, bringing in about $20,000 a year combined, they would increase their nest egg by about $50,000— assuming they spent some of their earnings on travel, which they would like to do.

3. Based on what you've learned in these few pages, you may start to make smarter financial decisions now that stand to benefit you down the line. For example, my husband and I were thinking of moving to a new town and renting for a year in order to see if we like the town. Now we're thinking more seriously of buying, because given what we know about this town, it's likely that even if we stayed for only two years, we'd get more for our money if we bought a home now rather than renting. That additional equity could go a long way to helping us catch up with our own retirement picture.

HOW DO YOU MANAGE THE MONEY YOU HAVE?

How are you doing so far? Is this stressful? Fun? A relief? Just keep reminding yourself of the greater happiness dividend: the pleasure of knowing you're getting your life under control now—and the comfort of knowing you'll enjoy more of the life you want in the future.

Now let's address another important way that money can make you happy: when you know your nest egg is growing steadily and your investments are thriving. I'm not an investment expert yet—although I'm working on it—but you don't need to be one to plan your own future and start making smart investments now.

This wasn't always the case. Just ten years ago you needed a fair amount of financial savvy to navigate the investment world. And while I encourage you to keep learning, these days it's possible to be a responsible, successful investor without understanding every last thing about P/E ratios and global markets.

Warning: If you like to gamble, if you like a challenge, if you like surprises and you secretly wish you could be a day trader—don't even read this section. Go immerse yourself in CNBC. This advice is for people who want a low-stress, low-risk, hands-off-yet-reliable way to grow their nest egg, which is what I recommend. Why? Not only because it's financially smart, but because by following a more easy-does-it method of investing, you'll be happier. According to a study by Swarthmore psychology professor Barry Schwartz of how choice can take a toll on well-being, most people are happier when they have fewer choices to contend with. The greater the number of choices, the more stress arises in making the "right" decision—and the more people are subject to doubt and regret over the option they do pick.

So unless you're comfortable playing the markets, or you

have the time and diligence to become a sophisticated investor, do yourself a favor and consider retirement strategies that minimize choice and maximize happiness.

The first is called **a life-cycle or targeted-maturity fund.** In the most basic terms, this is a basket of different investments that are rebalanced over time to provide you, the investor, with the best possible combination of growth (i.e., profit) and security as you get older. The idea is to put your money in at Point A and leave it there until Point B, when you retire. You don't do anything; the fund manager keeps track of how various sectors are performing, and with each passing year the manager gradually adjusts the mix of investments so that there's less risk but still plenty of gain, gradually pulling back on stocks and leaving more in bonds and cash.

Different investment companies like Vanguard, Fidelity, Charles Schwab, T. Rowe Price, and so on all offer these funds. The peculiar thing about the investment world is that every company uses a different name for the same type of fund. So what Vanguard calls a Life-Cycle Fund, Fidelity has branded a Freedom Fund. It's enough to make you pull your hair out, but don't sweat it. Time was you'd just buy a cup of coffee; now every twelve-year-old knows the difference between a macchiato and a frapuccino. In a very short time you'll find yourself at home with all the various terms. Call the 800 number and ask the customer service reps, most of whom are very obliging (because let's face it, they want your cash) and usually quite well informed.

To choose a fund, you could just pick one from a company that's known to be reliable (like Fidelity or Vanguard). If you're ready to do some comparison shopping, all you need is the ticker symbol of the funds you're considering and the Morningstar rating, which you can find at www.morningstar.com, or www.money.msn.com, or a variety of other Web sites. The Morningstar rating is the equivalent of the Good Housekeeping Seal of Approval or the Michelin stars for restaurants. Most financial Web sites offer fund analyses that are based on Morningstar data. If you think baseball statistics are complicated, you could get a migraine trying to interpret a single mutual fund report. So don't. Look at these three things instead:

- the ten-year performance
- how long the manager has been in place
- the Morningstar performance rating (given in stars; you want at least three stars, but more is better).

A NO-BRAINER WAY TO INVEST

The second method consists of what I call **user-friendly formulas.** One is called the Couch Potato method, and it was created by financial columnist Scott Burns, who writes for the *Dallas Morning News.* Another I mentioned earlier was invented by former broker Bill Schultheis and is called the Coffeehouse method (you can learn more at www.coffee houseinvestor.com).

These both rely on a similar passive-investing philosophy. That doesn't sound sexy—because it's not. If you really want to, you can get a PhD in the S&P 500 in order to invest—or you can follow a few simple, smart strategies, skip the complexities, lower your stress levels, and still make a good profit.

Both methods rely on **index funds**, which are mutual funds that mimic the performance of a certain stock market index. For example, the S&P 500 is an index of 500 very large companies. The performance of that index is a broad way to measure how the overall market is doing. An index fund based on the S&P 500 will perform just as well—and just as poorly—as those companies do. Why would you want to invest in a fund that's just a carbon copy of one part of the market? Because over time, the S&P 500 has an excellent rate of return. In the last fifty years, the average yield is 12 percent. That's far from record-breaking, but it's the kind of solid return you want when you're a novice investor who nonetheless wants steady profits.

So rather than trouble yourself picking a bunch of individual mutual funds, you can base your portfolio on index funds—as these two are—because an index fund is going to cover a full segment of the market and thus get some winners and some losers. But by and large, these tend to perform well over time. And the fees are very low.

GO TO A PRO

If you'd rather not get into asset allocation, the relative merits of stocks, bonds, real estate, foreign investments, and so forth, you might want to hire a fee-only financial planner (www.napfa.org can help you find a planner in your area; the

Sheryl Garrett network offers planners that charge only by the hour—www.garrettplanningnetwork.com). In fact, even if you do all the work yourself, you might want to hire someone to double-check your math and help you navigate around three big retirement potholes:

1. **Taxes:** If all your money is in a tax-deferred account like a 401(k), you won't need to worry about whether your portfolio is tax-efficient. But if you have additional IRAs, that may be something to ask an adviser. And unless you've invested all your retirement funds in a Roth, you also need to figure out how much you're going to pay in taxes on all your withdrawals, including your Social Security benefits. Although your tax rate in retirement will be lower than your current one, taxes can erode your savings. Consulting with a professional now can help you preserve more of your cash for yourself, rather than have Uncle Sam take it.

2. **Fees:** Assuming you'd rather not lose tens of thousands of dollars in retirement money for no reason, get a professional to assess the fees that are attached to your investments. Fees are the privilege we all pay for being able to invest our cash in the market, like the entry fee at an amusement park. But if you're unaware of how they work and how quickly they can add up, account fees and management fees and transfer fees and loads can take a big, greedy bite out of your savings. For example, Terri and Mark's final nest egg of $780,000 assumes a 1 percent fee is being de-

ducted during their thirty-year savings period. That's very low. But if they were unlucky enough to have investments that cost them 2 percent a year, which is very possible, their nest egg would drop by almost $100,000.

3. **Withdrawal Rates:** When you leave a job and retire, the entire contents of your 401(k) are rolled over into an account that you can now access. While in some cases there is a mandatory withdrawal age—you have to start at seventy or pay a penalty—*there is no mandatory amount.* No one is going to hand you a "paycheck" each week or each month. It's up to you. You can set it up so that you get a check in the same amount sent at regular intervals, just like a salary, but the truth is that retirement withdrawals are on the honor system.

A GREAT START

Even if it takes you a total of several hours to complete all the steps in this chapter, that's a minor investment for a huge gain in terms of present and future peace of mind.

· Now you have a much clearer idea of what sort of life you might want when you retire.
· You've thought about what that lifestyle would cost.
· Now you have some idea of what size nest egg you need.

- And you know what you need to save in order to reach that nest egg.
- You've got some good ideas about how to invest your money, or how to hire a pro to help you do so.
- Despite the natural uncertainty that veils the future, you can now enjoy a well-earned sense of financial control, and satisfaction.

Now let's have some fun!

10

Boost Your Fun Yields

Money is better than poverty,
if only for financial reasons.

—Woody Allen

What role should fun play in your happiness portfolio? That may sound like a silly question, but according to financial portfolio theory—a well-known investment model—you need certain sectors that will perform when the market is up, and a separate group that will boost your returns when the market is down. So in investment terms, having fun is the asset that you can rely on to keep your spirits steady, no matter what's going on in the rest of your life. Thus, I not only recommend investing in frivolous amusement for its own sake (the original purpose, I believe), but because it's a hedge against life's inevitable crashes.

There's a large body of research on the benefits of laughter, a fair amount on the so-called study of leisure (now that sounds like a relaxing field), but it's a little harder to unearth scientific support for the relationship between having fun and being happy. Which makes sense, I suppose, since studying whether having fun makes you happy is like pondering whether water makes you wet. (That said, research by French neurologists indicates that apparently time does fly when you're having fun. Good to know. I think a more interesting area of research would be whether champagne does make you giggle more, but that's just me.)

Sex is another story. There are loads of studies on sex, and because as we all know sex is a pretty big source of fun, perhaps searching for the evidence linking sex to happiness could be seen as a reason to have more fun—and sex. As you may recall from a study I mentioned in the introduction, when nine hundred women in Texas were asked to list the activities that were most satisfying in their day, sex was number one.

Moreover, in another fairly recent study, economists David Blanchflower and Andrew Oswald reviewed surveys of more than sixteen thousand Americans, comparing self-reports of sexual activity and happiness with other economic data. By extraordinary mathematical gymnastics that only economists can do, they arrived at the remarkable conclusion that not only does having more sex definitely make you happier (we knew that), but increasing the frequency of your sex life from once a month to once a week is the equivalent of getting a $50,000 windfall. See, it's even more fun than you thought.

In any case, taking one three-letter word as a stand-in for the other, this study seems to suggest that we should all invest in having lots of playful, intimate, loving, physical fun because, whether it feels like a $500 or a $50,000 windfall to you, it can only add to your happiness portfolio over time.

A SURVEY IS BORN

Still, as a journalist, it's hard to proceed in writing an entire chapter without showing any solid evidence on which to base it. So I decided to conduct a Highly Unscientific (Yet Groundbreaking) National Fun Survey of anyone who would answer my e-mails about the nature of fun and how to have more of it. For purposes of replicating my results, like-minded researchers might want to conduct this survey themselves. You can answer it yourself now, pose it to members of your household or office, or send it out via e-mail. It consists of one question, so it's relatively easy—and the results are surprising. The question was: *If you could do three things that would add more fun to your life, what would they be?*

My hypothesis was twofold: (1) Most people would know exactly how to increase their fun quotient, and (2) most people would list activities that were (a) affordable and (b) within the scope of their current lives. And of course I was curious to know how many people were actually doing any of the fun things they listed.

Method: Twenty-nine subjects responded to a single-question e-mail survey about fun; thirteen were men and sixteen were women. They ranged in age from twenty-six to eighty. I don't think they were a representative sample of any particular group. The margin of error was really small, because why would anyone lie about this stuff?

Results: About 98 percent of those surveyed responded immediately with their fun wish list—indicating they knew perfectly well what they'd love to do to increase their fun yields. About 79 percent of those activities were affordable. Things like buying a "peacock blue Vespa," traveling abroad, quitting one's job, or getting Yankee season tickets I counted as being rather large expenditures, but these were rare. So my first two hypotheses were confirmed: Most people know how to have more fun and can afford to do so. But I was discouraged to learn (although not terribly surprised) that 58 percent of people weren't doing any of the things they listed—even though in most cases these were within their reach.

> **Action may not always bring happiness; but there is no happiness without action.** —*Benjamin Disraeli*

Here is a sample of the things people had on their fun lists. I share these with you not just for your own inspiration, but so you can marvel—as I did—at the simple things that people say would increase their joie de vivre. Yet many of these are things they're simply not doing, or haven't done yet.

- Playing more games like Pictionary, Cranium, or even Charades with other adults
- Going to a karaoke bar—not to sing, but to watch ("I think it would be hilarious," wrote one woman, adding that her husband refused to support this quest.)

- Brewing beer
- Hiking
- Reading a good book at sundown and then napping before dinner
- People-watching at a coffee shop while eavesdropping on nearby conversations ("A shameful activity I relish shamelessly!" one woman confessed.)
- Seeing more live theater
- Going to the opera
- Hosting potluck dinners so as to see more friends
- Renting an RV and touring the West
- Finishing a children's book
- Going to a classy bar once a week to have a perfect martini and do some people-watching
- Taking cooking classes
- Spending more time with one's spouse
- Going somewhere new on a regular basis, whether it's a restaurant, museum, storytelling night, or weekend destination
- Showing up at a party or dinner in a costume ("Dressing up is fun for everyone," wrote one guy.)

The number one most-wished-for source of fun, from 24 percent of respondents (drrrrumroll, please):

- Going out dancing ("Find a great place, with great music, grab your partner, and just go—you're never too old for this," wrote one woman.)

The second most desired type of fun (17 percent):

· Having more free time, downtime, flex time

And to my great surprise—was everyone lying or just being shy?—only one person admitted they'd like to have more sex.

> **The Constitution only gives people the right to pursue happiness. You have to catch it yourself.** —*Anonymous*

The other major insight provided by my survey is that almost nobody said that having fun depended on buying stuff. People wanted to spend money doing things, seeing friends, learning something—yes. But aside from the wish for a screened-in porch, a motorcycle, bike, or scooter, single-malt scotch, and the like, what most respondents desired was based on action and experience and being with people, not having things.

So if you're operating at a fun deficit—which according to my survey approximately 58 percent of people are—there are three basic tools you need in order to increase your fun yields: (1) a list, and (2) a plan, and (3) a partner in crime, if not a posse.

If this sounds too clinical, too structured, and not at all fun—relax. According to the most fun people I interviewed, that is, those most successful at having the sort of spontaneous enjoyment of life we all crave, their big secret is to leave nothing to chance. Here is a three-point strategy from a high-spirited PR woman who enlivens the social scene on at least two continents and literally has more fun than anyone I know. (In fact, it can be painful to have a conversation with her, because she is always en route to an event far more fun than whatever I'm doing that week.)

1. **Put the word out.** Let anyone and everyone know that you want to hear about interesting events, opportunities, celebrations large and small, free concerts, sports events, etc.

2. **Get plugged in.** Put yourself on mailing lists of your favorite organizations, theater groups, lecture clubs, art galleries, museums, your local alumni group, etc. Join a group that will get you doing fun stuff that's hard to plan on your own (ski trips, camping, ballroom dancing, gardening, etc).

3. **Plan, plan, plan!** Find people who are equally committed to getting the most fun out of life and hook up with them. Be ready and willing to make room in your schedule for more fun, even—or maybe especially—if it means postponing something tedious.

FUN AT ANY PRICE

Putting your resources into fun is probably one of the least expensive ways you can boost your happiness returns. True, there's no limit to how much you can spend on various forms of entertainment, but did former Tyco exec Dennis Kozlowski really have that much fun when he spent over a million bucks on procuring Jimmy Buffett and nudie ice sculptures for his wife's birthday in Italy? I don't know, I wasn't there. But I think the key is to invest in what you love to do, not splurge on some fleeting extravagance.

Of course, the occasional foray into high-priced frivolity can be fabulous. Stephanie, twenty-seven, who works in marketing in Chicago, decided to spend a $3,000 chunk of her bonus on a one-week stay at the Ritz in Jamaica last year. "My husband and I worked so hard all winter, and we barely saw each other. So when I heard about this package deal, I just *had* to do it!" And a very happy decision that turned out to be. "We lived it up, every penny's worth of that three grand," she says.

While a onetime splurge can certainly add to your stash of happiness, my feeling is that it's more effective to invest regularly in your fun sector. Vince, thirty, has bought season tickets to attend University of Maryland football games since he graduated. And he still flies back to attend each game—even though he now lives in Florida. "I know it's a crazy way to spend money, but I love it," he says. He stays with friends who are also big fans, "and I usually get enough frequent flyer miles to earn one free ticket a season," he says.

On the other hand, Steve, sixty—the guy who bought the Jaguar, remember?—spends nothing to visit with three octogenarian neighbors each week, asking them about their lives and recollections of the Rhode Island town they all live in, and taking notes for a possible book.

Of course, you've now read enough of this book to know that it's not about how much money you have, but how and where and why you spend it. And as my Highly Unscientific (Yet Groundbreaking) National Fun Survey revealed, you don't need to spend much to increase your fun yields. Often it's not the cash that's lacking, but the inspiration. One woman whose fun list included renting a beach house on the coast of Alabama, where she grew up, e-mailed me after she answered the survey to say that she realized how easy it would be to go ahead and fulfill her wish. As of this writing, she and her husband have rented that beach house. "Thank you for sparking that idea!" she wrote.

The sparks are all around us, of course. If you want to invest in having more fun, the surest way is to keep your own wish list updated—and handy. Post it on the fridge or carry an index card in your pocket or purse. That way you avoid the video store dilemma of suddenly forgetting what you want the minute you try to remember it.

TRY IT, YOU'LL LIKE TRYING

Here are some other ways to boost your fun quotient, drawing on what we've discussed throughout the previous chapters:

- Nearly all the survey results show that having fun = doing new things (or at the very least, doing *something*). Turn back to chapter 5, "Invest in Yourself," or the happiness list from chapter 1, and find new fun investments there.
- Do a cost-benefit analysis: Having dinner with friends is fun. But for that same $30 you might spend, what about attending a baseball game, a day at a carnival, a night at the opera? When it comes to fun, the choice is yours.

- Save time for fun. Review the ideas in chapter 4 and see if you can buy yourself some time to have more fun this week—perhaps by hiring a sitter, housecleaner, or lawn mower. Even dropping off your laundry at the Fluff 'n' Fold will net you a couple of hours that you can invest in more rewarding diversions.
- Put fun first in your day, your week, your life. Sometimes the more "serious" things in life must take precedence—but not every day. Remember that we want a balanced portfolio here, and having well-established sources of fun not only enriches your life now, but provides some needed bounce when the chips are falling where they may.

The Name of the Game Is Exploration

If reading this chapter has given you a hankering to have more fun in your own life—good! Sometimes fun just happens, and those moments are magical, but by and large you have to keep things fresh with a stream of enticing ideas and resources. (I've found that if you do the same stuff too often, it deteriorates into "nice," which is fine, but it's not fun.) When my daily routine starts to exhibit signs of fun deprivation—I get excited by the idea of getting out . . . to the grocery store—it helps to hear what mischief other people are up to. I got a few people to dish about their diversions:

- Beth, 41, from a few chapters back, gets a kick from: "Skipping stones across water. Making your child belly laugh. Fireworks! Finding cool knitting patterns on the

Internet—and pumpkin-carving patterns too, believe it or not. Taking road trips to somewhere new or nostalgic—and skinny-dipping and other acts of exhibitionism."

- My friend Kurt, 44, an artist in New York, advocates boat rides ("They're surprisingly fun"); fingerpainting and other crafts (check out www.craftster.com); sneaking onto a golf course at night; and "having more fun sex." He says, "Try Polaroids. Have a tickle fight. Wear a nurse's costume. Or play strip chess! For even more fun, assign articles of clothing to the pieces. Last fun thing," he adds, "make a little movie. Everybody has a digital camera now that shoots video. It's way more fun than watching other people's videos."

- Stephanie, 27, who took the trip to Jamaica and clearly knows from fun, is a big fan of reading the free satirical weekly paper *The Onion*. "They also have numerous podcasts on iTunes," she says, "or try www.collegehumor.com." She also recommends getting an earful of Flight of the Conchords, a group that bills itself as "New Zealand's fourth most popular guitar-based digi-bongo a capella-rap-funk-comedy folk duo." Check them out at: www.conchords.co.nz or www.whatthefolk.net.

Last, but definitely not least, my go-getter sister-in-law, Deirdre, contributed this trove of ideas:

- "Find local farms that let you pick your own! It's fun, but don't pick anything smaller than an apple—too many scratches and bug bites.

- "Rent or borrow a TV series you missed. Right now we are Netflixing our way through *Six Feet Under* and we will start on *Deadwood* after that. You can also get all those great 'Britcoms' and mysteries on Netflix, too. British TV alone could keep you entertained for a year.

- "This is going to sound lame, but, hit the library! Our main library has revolving art shows with local artists, book discussion groups, lectures, readings, and an awesome collection of videos, DVDs, books on tape and CDs . . . plus, you can do a little kissin' in the stacks, too. We go there a lot.

- "Find out what your local teams are and go to some games. We have minor league baseball and hockey teams and they are great fun that won't kill your budget.

- "Oh, and don't forget the good old Saturday-afternoon wine tastings at your local wine shop!"

You know, it was so much fun asking people what they do for fun, it was hard to stop—but I'm sure you get the idea. In fact, you might want to add that as question number two when you conduct your own Highly Unscientific Fun Survey. Either way, I encourage you to keep up ongoing research, noting which investments seem to bring the most to this key sector of your portfolio. Remember, if you follow the 60% Solution money organizing plan, a full 10 percent of your gross income should be spent on pure frivolity. This will come in handy for the next chapter, too, which is about giving more to the people who matter most to you.

11

Enrich Your Relationships

True happiness . . . arises, in the first place, from enjoyment of oneself; and, in the next, from friendship and conversation of a few select companions.

—*Joseph Addison*

We all place great value on our relationships. Why write a chapter about how to "enrich" them when it's one of those truths we all hold to be self-evident? If you knit together every book, magazine article, television show, and aphorism from Dr. Phil that offered relationship advice, you could put a poncho on Pluto. Are further instructions necessary?

Yes. Despite the fact that we all know how important various people are to us, how they enrich our lives in a myriad of ways, the demands of life are at odds with our need to maintain those bonds. Many if not most people feel chronically short of the sort of time, money, and energy we know our relationships deserve. We're tapped out, time-crunched, overstressed, and overextended—so there's a tendency to slip into basic-maintenance mode, do the minimum required, show up when we have to, send a card when we can't, and let e-mail do the rest.

"I'm doing the best I can" is the prevailing excuse, with "She will understand" as a close runner-up, and "We'll do something *great* on his birthday" in third place.

When you're running late and have only twenty minutes to work out at the gym, doing your best is acceptable. We can't afford to give our relationships such short shrift. One of the most powerful ways to increase every level of happiness in your life—from basic contentment to sheer bliss—is to invest in the people who matter most to you.

Perhaps you think it sounds mercenary or self-serving to reverse the standard equation and focus on how your relationships can benefit *you.* Of course, it's good and right and admirable to give unto others, but there's nothing wrong with acknowledging the beauty of this particular two-way street: The more you invest in those you care about, the richer your own life will be. And the more people who take this self-nourishing cycle seriously, perhaps, the more society itself may benefit. A few years ago Robert Putnam's book *Bowling Alone* detailed the erosion of social bonds—and the price we pay in loneliness and the loss of close personal connections.

> **People think love is an emotion. Love is good sense.**
>
> —*Ken Kesey*

Likewise, Canadian economist John Helliwell is one of a small but growing number of researchers who believe that investing in "social capital" is important on a personal and political level, for the well-being of all. Whereas people's sense of being connected to one another rose for most of the twentieth century, in some Western countries like Canada and the United States it has declined in the last thirty years—a dispiriting trend that many economists, psychologists, sociologists, and spiritual leaders (never mind people like you and me) connect to the escalating levels of unhappiness and emptiness that plague modern life. In a sad and unsettling report published by *American Sociological Review* in 2006, researchers found that the average person has only two friends they would count as close confidants, down from three in 1985. And the number of people who said they didn't have even one person they could confide in rose to 25 percent, from 10 percent in 1985.

This is particularly disturbing when you consider that we reap tremendous gains from the various bonds in our lives.

- In one study, Dr. Helliwell asked people to assign a dollar amount to various relationships in order to have a more concrete way to measure their value. Respondents felt that joining an organization was estimated to be worth about $25,000; the value of seeing family frequently was worth about $125,000, and seeing friends often was worth $100,000.
- In repeated studies, people who rate themselves happiest with their lives report having strong social ties. In 2002, psychologists Ed Diener and Martin Seligman published a study about the behavior of very happy people and found that they described themselves as more

extroverted, and as having more social and romantic relationships, than those who were less happy.

· And let's not forget the extraordinary gains that accrue to those who are married or involved in a long-term relationship. In a 2002 literature review entitled "The Extraordinary Effects of Marriage," economist Andrew Oswald noted that marriage is associated with living longer, with better mental health, and with lower rates of depression—oh, and it might even make you richer. "In virtually every country ever studied," Dr. Oswald writes, "workers who are married earn between 10 percent and 20 percent more than those who are single."

Isn't it possible that happier people tend to get married? Or that happier people tend to have more friends, not the other way around? Of course. But either way, you stand to gain, if you'll forgive the pun, by putting your money, time, and energy into the bonds in your relationship portfolio.

PUT PEOPLE FIRST

This is what many people assume they're doing already. But in a study called "Chasing the Good Life," economics researcher Anke Zimmerman demonstrates that our relationships may be taking more of a backseat than we realize. Whereas it's been well documented that, over time, most people's desire for material goods increases (a swimming pool, vacation home, more money), Zimmerman found that, in contrast, most people's desire for personal goods (a happy marriage, good health, children) remains steady or decreases slightly over the life cycle. This doesn't mean that people become less interested in having a happy marriage, for example, but whereas our desire for stuff only escalates with time and age and income, the value of more personal satisfactions tends to be constant in our eyes.

> **You are forgiven for your happiness and your successes only if you generously consent to share them.**
>
> —*William Blake*

This led Zimmerman to speculate that perhaps we are in danger of undermining our own happiness—because while many people continue to "chase the good life" via second homes and designer clothes and higher incomes, we don't do the same in our personal lives. "As a result," she writes, "most individuals spend a disproportionate amount of time working, and sacrifice family life and health, domains in which aspirations remain fairly constant as actual circumstances change, and where attainment of one's goals has a more lasting impact on happiness."

What's interesting about Zimmerman's analysis is that she's capturing a pattern of wants, as revealed through a survey of thousands of Americans over a twenty-five-year period. The study isn't about who *gets* the bigger income or the swimming pool, but what people say they *aspire* to in this life. What Zimmerman is suggesting is that once people's personal aspirations are satisfied, those then get overshadowed by the ever-louder drumbeat of material wants, and people run the risk of not investing enough in the less conspicuous domains that sustain them. In other words, if you were asked whether you considered your relationships a priority, you'd probably say: Absolutely! But if you look at how you distribute your time, energy, and money—I wonder what you'd see?

Given that everyone's resources are limited, you need to exercise some discretion in this sector of your portfolio. You know which relationships contribute the most to your well-being, which people add the most to your life. You can't divest yourself of every single unrewarding relationship. There are many people to whom we're bonded for reasons that have little to do with happiness. But that shouldn't stop you from investing more in those who have the greatest potential to bring you pleasure. Here's how:

1. Spend Money on People

Like most couples, Elizabeth and Vince have reached a few financial compromises, one of them being that they each get a certain amount to spend per month at their own discretion. Vince typically spends his money on season tickets to football games at his alma mater, as I mentioned earlier. "And that's fine—it's his favorite thing," says Elizabeth. "The one place where I spend most of my money is on going out—because I'm the type of person who believes that when you have a friend, you have to see them once a week or every other week at the least. I spend my money on people."

Elizabeth says her friend focus has not changed one iota in

recent years, even though her budget was radically reduced after she went from working full-time in Washington, D.C., to studying for her master's in public administration in Florida. "The main difference is that now I try to spend six dollars instead of sixty when I go out," she says. "But for me the ultimate sacrifice would be not seeing my friends."

It's not the amount of money that matters, but the decision to put it toward those you care about that makes a huge difference. When Gus, thirty-eight, moved from the United States to Europe for a job, he invested about $30 a month to have an Internet telephone service installed in addition to the expensive local landline in his new home. "It was a hassle to set up, and paying for high-speed Internet here isn't cheap," he says, but this service made calls back home so much easier that the energy and expense were more than worth it. "Not only could I call my friends and family, they could reach me for the cost of a local call in the U.S."

These decisions may seem like no-brainers, but don't discount the impact of thinking like a real investor when it comes to using your money to enrich your connections to the most important people in your life.

- Review the expenses chart you made in chapter 2 with an eye toward how much you're spending on the people who make you happiest.
- Reallocate funds from less satisfactory areas of your life to increase the cash flow toward the people you value most, for example:

- Ditch Direct TV in order to go out more often with your spouse or a dear friend.
- For what you'd save by bringing your lunch to work, you could throw a great dinner party once a month.
- Reevaluate your spending blind spots. One woman admitted to me that in one year she spent 10 percent of her gross income on clothing. Whether clothes or gadgets are your weakness, funnel half of your indulgence money toward visiting your sister, treating a friend who can't afford to visit you, or taking your kids on a special outing.
- Weigh different investment strategies. When my father retired and moved to New Mexico—a move that took our Northeast-based family by surprise—plane tickets became a sudden but essential new budget item, and my husband and I had to come up with ways to afford to visit him. Our favorite strategy has been to save every five-dollar bill we get each day in a coffee can, which is a surprisingly quick and painless way to come up with extra cash for cross-country trips.

2. Invest Your Time

A few years ago Jerry, sixty, was a top salesman at one of the biggest car dealerships in New England. A former lawyer, Jerry says that the money he was making in sales trumped his relatively modest attorney's salary. "The popular concept is that lawyers are filthy rich, but that's not true," he says. The only trouble was that he was working eighty hours a week, six days a week, "and on Sundays I slept." Not surprisingly, his wife sat him down one day and said, "It's either the job or the marriage."

After six years as one of the top-earning salesmen in the region, Jerry didn't have to think too hard. He quit the job in order to invest in his marriage and since then has continued to work a more flexible schedule—which also affords him enough free time to visit his only daughter when he feels like it. "That's what really makes me happy," he says.

Here are some other ways to redistribute your time so more of it gets invested in people you care about:

- Hire a babysitter for an evening, an afternoon, or just a few hours so you can have some one-on-one time with your other children, your mate, or anyone else who brings you joy.
- Buy a plane ticket, train ticket, or rent-a-car so you can attend a wedding, shower, bar mitzvah, or other event that helps you stay connected to important people.
- A long weekend, a long lunch, or even just leaving work early can be a great way to make time for people you love to see, even if you're not paid for the time off.
- If you have kids, offer to swap a few hours of child care with a parent who is willing to do the same for you. You each get a breather, and the priceless comfort of knowing your safety net is bigger than you thought.
- If you're sitting on a stash of vacation time, allocate some of it to quick "getaways" that can even be stay-at-homes with the people you need to reconnect with.

3. Tap Your Resources

Margaret and Ian weren't always as successful as they are now ("In grad school we survived on rice and ramen," Ian says). So for several years it was hard for Margaret to scrape together the time and the money to travel from Tampa to Virginia to see her family. But ever since Ian's business took off a couple of years ago, the two have figured out a way to have a big family vacation once a year. "We have a friend who owns a big house and a boat down in the Keys," says Margaret, thirty-six. "So we rent out their house, and invite all the aunts and uncles and cousins down for a week every summer. We ask everyone to contribute something—for food and gas for the boat—but we cover the rest," she says. "It's just a great way to see all these people we love, sit around eating spaghetti and hanging out on the boat, for a solid week. It's gotten to be a habit and a tradition that we treasure."

It may take a little finagling, or some creative calculus on your part, but most of us have resources we can use to enrich our relationships, many of which require only a modest expenditure:

- Use a business trip to catch up with a college buddy.
- Spend frequent flyer miles to bring someone close to you.
- Build a blog so your old friends can stay in contact.
- Host a family reunion, holiday, or graduation party.
- If you live in a "destination" city, encourage those you love (and still enjoy at close quarters!) to visit for a few days.

4. *Do* Sweat the Small Stuff

My life is a junkyard of discarded grand gestures—big, beautiful things I was going to do for so-and-so, to show them how much I cared, how grateful I was, how much what they did meant to me. Bold moves may not be your weakness, but if they are, consider trading them in for smaller, more regular displays of affection. Otherwise you risk doing nothing at all. So if your resources are limited, investing even a little bit into action makes all the difference. Because when it comes to nurturing the people who are most important to you, it's not the thought that counts. Sorry. It's the doing. Even the smallest gesture of caring can go a long way toward sustaining strong bonds.

- You don't need to send a big bouquet you can't afford when a simple thank-you card would be just as welcome.
- You don't need to sweep your spouse away for a weekend when a dinner out would make them feel just as loved.
- Last summer Tricia, forty, a single mom who lives in Pennsylvania, wanted to take her kids to Disneyland, but didn't have the money. "So I took them camping," she says. And for about $25 a day, they had one of the best family trips ever.
- If you can't afford to fly across the country to visit a friend who's getting divorced, getting married, or having a baby, pick the next best thing, even if it seems like the least best thing. Send a postcard. Pick up the phone. Text message her once a day. Send the funniest piece of

spam you get this week, with a personal note saying, "Hi, I'm thinking of you."

5. Invest in Community

When Rachel and Mark, a couple in their fifties, moved out of New York City to give their two children a more comfortable upbringing in a New Jersey suburb, within a year they realized their mistake. It wasn't their home, "which was absolutely gorgeous," says Rachel. It was being far from the community they loved in New York, and the synagogue they had belonged to for years.

So they moved back. There were a number of factors that drove them to change their minds—and homes—again. In fact, for the few years they lived in New Jersey, Rachel says, they remained members of their old synagogue and would try to drive in for services from time to time—or cart their kids to and from after-school activities—but it soon grew too stressful. "When we moved away, we didn't appreciate what an important part of our lives this community was, but once we did, we decided it was worth it to move again."

Although you can imagine the financial and emotional hassle of reversing their move, Rachel says that being able to attend services every week and rejoin community activities has been an incalculable blessing for the whole family.

Fortunately, most of us won't have to make such an elaborate change in order to build more of a community network. Often the channels are in place; you just have to put more into making the connection.

- **Invest in local issues.** My husband and I didn't really feel a part of our community in upstate New York until we got involved in planning, zoning, and environmental issues in our area. Attending meetings and being more plugged in requires more time than money usually, but it's turned out to be a terrific investment in our quality of life.

- **Find your crowd.** The Internet is either blamed for fostering social isolation or praised for being a great connector. Really, it's up to you. Services like meetup.org and friendster.com can help you join a group of kindred souls who will understand your desire to save the spotted wombat or find a decent eighties DJ, and often it won't set you back more than the cost of a meal. Or spend a little more to join a club devoted to an activity you love (off-road kayaking, anyone?).

- **Find faith.** Religious and spiritual groups offer many ways to join their communities. Ellen, forty-eight, who lives in Ann Arbor, decided to join a Bible study group with a friend a couple of years ago. She's not super-religious, "but reading the Bible and understanding it is something I've always wanted to do." The classes were inexpensive, but the social gains were immense, she says. "Who knew I'd end up being connected to such kind and interesting people?"

- **Remember your alma mater.** Alumni organizations are an abundant source of connections—and maybe even some fond memories of your senior year. The dues are usually low, and often you get alumni privileges or discounts—which is nothing compared to the priceless opportunity to reminisce about the meal plan.

The next chapter is about taking some of these connections to the next level and learning the benefits of investing in the wider world.

12

Gain by Giving

Do your little bit of good where you are; it's those little bits of good put together that overwhelm the world.

—*Archbishop Desmond Tutu*

I s giving supposed to feel good to the giver? This may not sound like the basis for a controversy, but the field of philanthropy has been thrown into a state of flux thanks to a spate of recent research that provides strong evidence for the fact that altruism not only benefits those who receive, but it bestows extraordinary benefits on the giver.

This sounds like good news for everyone—and it is. But the traditional model of philanthropy is still very much grounded in the idea that one should give because of the merits of a certain organization or the needs of the population being served. "It was a scolding model," says Dwight Burlingame, author of a three-volume encyclopedia *Philanthropy in America*.

In philanthropic parlance, this older approach is called the

demand-side model—and as you may remember, it was epito-
mized years ago by actress Sally Struthers's woeful appeals, in
magazine ads and on TV, to *pleeeeease* give a few cents a day to
feed a child. The growing trend today is to shift to "supply-
side" tactics, which emphasize "the joy of giving," Burlingame
says.

And joyful it can be—and healthy, too, apparently. By doing
magnetic resonance imaging on certain areas of the brain,
Colin Camerer, a professor of economics at the California University of Technology, has found that altruism kicks off activity
in one of the brain's pleasure and reward centers. Meanwhile, a
growing number of other scientists has found that those who
volunteer reduce their risk of mortality by 40 to 60 percent—
and helping others is also linked to better physical and mental
health. Interestingly, those who received help did not get the
same benefits.

Of course, there's nothing wrong with giving because you
think it's right, or because you support a certain organization's
mission. But this new area of scientific inquiry seems to support the idea that by becoming a more active giver, you stand to
boost the performance of your happiness portfolio as well.

SPENDERS AND GIVERS

Americans are big givers. In 2004, charitable giving in the
United States reached a record high of $248 billion, with $187
billion of that coming from individuals, according to the annual *Giving USA* report—and that's just cash and donated goods.

It doesn't include volunteer time, services, or donating blood, for example. According to Linda Lampkin, a researcher at the National Center for Charitable Statistics (NCCS), "Most people who volunteer also give. It's not an either-or situation."

Yet giving as a percentage of disposable income, adjusted for inflation, has hovered at or near 2 percent for almost forty years. So although individuals did give more in 2004, it was roughly the same percentage of their disposable cash as it has been for decades: about 2 percent. Like many others in this field, Burlingame, who is also the associate executive director of the Center on Philanthropy at Indiana University, believes that a greater emphasis on joy-based giving could increase the bounty of philanthropic activity in this country.

> **All of us are born for a reason, but all of us don't discover why. Success in life has nothing to do with what you gain in life or accomplish for yourself. It's what you do for others.**
>
> —*Danny Thomas*

This notion comes from studies of what motivates people to give as well as research in the field of social biology, which has found that even other primates exhibit "giving" behavior—and that this behavior benefits the health of the individual as well as the species. Stephanie Brown, a psychologist who studies altruism at the University of Michigan, is one of the leading researchers in this field. She and her father published a paper in 2006 posing a new theory of how altruism stems from the evolution of more complex social bonds. "Essentially, if people engage in altruistic behavior toward one another, they are more likely to cultivate interdependence on one another," she said in an interview.

So although the most obvious purpose of philanthropy is to benefit others, the greater function of developing habits of altruism may be to bring people closer and create a greater sense of connection and happiness in our own lives as well. Despite all the shortcomings built into human nature, our one great strength is the ability to feel immense pleasure the more we connect to other people and to the things we find meaningful in life. Like many before him, psychologist Martin Seligman feels passionately that "the exercise of virtue" is one of the core types of happiness. While we live in a world that seems to rely on every possible shortcut to happiness—from sensual pleasures to psychotropic drugs—a different sort of happiness can be found when we exercise our best selves, our greatest strengths.

He's not suggesting we have to give up the shortcuts, but that we make some effort to reach for rewards that lie beyond easy, feel-good moments. In his bestselling book *Authentic Happiness*, Seligman describes an informal experiment he conducted with some students: During the course of a week, each person had to engage in one pleasurable activity and one philanthropic act, and then write about the result.

"The results were life-changing," he writes. "The afterglow of the 'pleasurable' activity (hanging out with friends, or watching a movie, or eating a hot fudge sundae) paled in comparison with the effects of the kind action." One student described how she helped her third-grade nephew with his math, and "for the rest of the day, I could listen better, I was mellower, and people liked me much more than usual."

Seligman calls the exercise of kindness and compassion a "gratification" as opposed to a pleasure, because "it calls on your strengths to rise to an occasion and meet a challenge."

There are plenty of times when you act out of kindness and there's no such "afterglow." There's nothing like doing a favor for a friend that's inconvenient for you to leave the weird taste of virtue and resentment in your mouth. I'm not arguing that all charitable gestures ought to be convenient, but what these new studies suggest is that you're more likely to feel that uplifting feeling when you're not just acting out of kindness, but out of a sense of your own philanthropic identity: with a sense of meaning or that this action is important to you. Your own giving habits today may be passionate or indifferent, but if thus far you've thought of philanthropy only as giving to others, here are some ways to think about the kind of giving that might provide a deeper gratification that enriches you—as well as those to whom you give.

> **The smallest good deed is better than the grandest good intention.**   —*Duguet*

1. Let the Spirit Move You

When Jack and Mona adopted a baby from Guatemala a few years ago, it opened their eyes to the plight of the many other children in that country who also need help. They found an organization through which they could sponsor a three-year-old girl who was disabled and thus far less likely ever to be adopted.

By giving just $38 a month, they enabled the little girl to be moved out of her orphanage and placed in a foster home, where she received much better care.

Although Mona and Jack are in their forties, they admitted that this was a fairly new experience for them. "Until we got a bit older and things 'happened' in our lives, we didn't have a whole lot of incentive—or money, frankly—to do much for anyone other than ourselves," Mona says. But after adopting their son, they realized how much it would mean to them both to feel that they were contributing something to a cause they now felt personally invested in. "It makes us feel less helpless, and it keeps us connected to the place where our daughter is from," she says.

- **Know your issues.** If an illness, event, or political issue has had a major impact on your life—cancer, suicide, sudden infant death syndrome, elder care, environmental cleanup—use your personal knowledge to find the most meaningful way that you can give.
- **Let inspiration strike.** On the flip side, if you feel a strong connection to a cause outside your ken, use it as an opportunity to learn as well as give.

2. Give from Personal Experience

When Sherrie, fifty-five, was a federal employee, although she regularly donated to various charities via payroll deductions—she didn't really get that much pleasure out of "giving to a faceless organization," as she puts it. Now that she's in the private sector,

Sherrie has decided to give directly to kids in her area who need basic things like school supplies. "At Christmas you can pick a kid's name off a tree and get them what they've wished for," she says, "and at the start of school you can volunteer to buy a certain child all their school supplies."

That may not sound like a lifesaving endeavor, but it has enormous meaning to Sherrie, who grew up in a family that had constant money problems. "As the youngest in my family, I had hand-me-down *everything*, and I know what it feels like to pine away for cool new clothes or pens or anything to call your very own," she says. So she makes sure to pick out the best selection of stuff that's not just useful, but super kid-trendy. "I just love the idea of some less-than-privileged kid going to the first day of school with all their bling-bling supplies," she laughs. "I know what kids are like, and I know what a difference it can make if you have something like what everyone else does."

- **Share your expertise.** If you have a knack for math or love to swim, consider volunteering to teach underprivileged kids in your area. Many schools and other organizations offer mentoring or tutoring programs, and they need the skilled labor you can provide.
- **Target a local issue.** You don't have to contribute to a multinational cause to feel effective; investing in more grassroots efforts can feel just as meaningful. Does the high school need new basketball uniforms? Is there an asthma crisis in your area? Learn how you can make a difference in your own backyard.

3. Find a Comfortable Connection

Sonia, forty-five, admits that she used to donate more time when she was younger—now she just writes a check to the groups she wants to support. Besides the fact that many organizations prefer money, it's better for Sonia: "It's like instant gratification," she says. She read somewhere that by giving a small amount to places you believe in at the beginning and middle of every month—or once each paycheck, for most people—you start to feel even more active, involved, and, basically, like you're kicking some butt in the world.

- **Keep it simple.** Don't put pressure on yourself to show up at a soup kitchen if it's not your thing. Whether you give money to a cause once a month or donate time once a year—you'll be a more generous giver when you do what feels right for you.
- **Learn from others.** The next time you're with friends or family, crack open the conversation about how and why they give. The myriad ways people show their giving spirit is an excellent source of inspiration.

> **If you light a lamp for somebody, it will also brighten your path.** —*Buddhist saying*

4. Go Off the Beaten Path

Ned, a businessman in Florida, has seen his company take off in recent years—and he has used his greater economic reach to provide much-needed goods for communities in the Dominican Republic and Peru. He and his business partner have set up a foundation that collects donations from the U.S. and sends them along via small church groups and charities to be distributed in villages and towns where they're needed most.

"In a place like the Dominican Republic, they get hit just as hard as we do in Florida by the hurricane season, but they don't even have FEMA down there," says Ian, thirty-eight.

When he first came up with the idea of creating this donation network, he wasn't sure whether it would all come together. But he was surprised to discover the number of groups who travel to other countries with a mission to give; he decided that his part was to become a conduit to make sure those groups had the supplies they needed from Americans who were willing to give.

"We forget how rich we are here," he says. "I take old baseball gloves and jerseys that families here consider worn out—and kids down in D.R. can use that equipment for years."

- **Don't let headlines be your guide.** Long after Hurricane Katrina, the 2004 tsunami, and the genocide in the Sudan vanished from the front pages, people still needed help rebuilding their lives. Look beyond the news to see where your dollars are still needed.
- **Give someone a leg up.** Microlending programs, which support small businesses in developing areas, are some of the most successful not-for-profit programs around. You can give money or expertise.

5. Have Fun Giving

One charity that seems to have captured the minds and hearts of a lot of people these days is Heifer International (www.heifer.org). In addition to having a Web site packed with so many cute animal pictures you have to practically tear yourself away from it, the concept is biblically simple and irresistible.

Rather than give your money to a specific cause, Heifer International enables you to provide animals or livestock that will help people run their farm or ply their trade. In other words, for $250 you can buy a whole water buffalo ($25 gets you a "share" of one), which will be given to a farmer in Asia. A mere $30 gift will provide a family with a set of honeybees, a hive, and training in beekeeping—apparently an easy way to supplement or even generate an income.

Of course, you're not exactly buying live animals, as the Web site clarifies. You are contributing to Heifer's overall mission to give families not just temporary aid, but the means to support themselves. It's like a variation on the old proverb, "Give a man a fish and you feed him for a day. Buy him a water buffalo and he won't need to fish!"

- **Get your hands dirty.** Join Habitat for Humanity and get the hands-on reward of helping to build or repair someone's home (and learn valuable skills as well).
- **Tap local talent.** Host a fund-raiser for your favorite cause by putting on a play, a comedy night, or an art auction.

> If you have not often felt the joy of doing a kind act, you
> have neglected much, and most of all yourself.
>
> *—Anonymous*

These days there's a lot of concern about whether the organization you plan to get involved with is legitimate. Given that even big, household-name charities have been involved in scandals having to do with executive pay and how funds are distributed, it's only prudent to be wary of who gets your time, money, or even that old living room set. After all, the number of organizations that apply for tax-exempt status each year is in the tens of thousands, according to Bennett Weiner, chief operating officer of the BBB Wise Giving Alliance, a division of the Better Business Bureau. "In 1980 there were about 300,000 organizations that had received 501c3 tax-exempt status—today it's over a million," he says.

It's not that so many groups are out there fighting the good fight. It's that the tax-exempt status that spells "charity" to most of us—which is determined by section 501c3 of the IRS tax code—is rather broad, Weiner says. "There are twenty types of 'tax-exempt status,'" he notes, from charities to advocacy groups to unions, lobbying groups, and all kinds of benevolent organizations. Donating to those groups doesn't make your gift tax-deductible, for example, so you should always double-check with the organization, if claiming a tax deduction is your aim. Not all Americans give in order to deduct, however. Few people give enough to exceed the standard deduction and itemize their contributions. According to the Center on Philanthropy at Indiana University, there were some 69 million households that gave, but did not itemize and therefore couldn't claim a deduction.

GIVE BUT DON'T GET TAKEN

How do you determine whether the organization in question is aboveboard? Weiner says there are five common red flags to beware of:

1. Watch Out for Cases of Mistaken Identity

One clever ploy is for a fraudulent group to use a name that sounds familiar to get your dollars, e.g., "Houses for Humanity." Always double-check that you're giving to the place you had in mind.

2. Don't Give in to Pressure

When someone won't let you off the phone or keeps you on that street corner despite your attempts to walk away, "That's a ruse to get you to give without looking any farther," Weiner says. Don't buy it.

3. Beware of Sob Stories

"Watch out for overly emotional appeals that go on and on about a problem, but really don't tell you what the charity is doing," says Weiner. "Something may be amiss."

4. Don't Work Too Hard

The program's goals and methods should be stated clearly on whatever material you're given. "Watch out for vague program descriptions," says Weiner. "You shouldn't have to be Sherlock Holmes to find out what they do."

5. Don't Assume It's a Charity

Lots of nonprofits need donations of money or time, but they may not be considered charitable organizations under the law.

Weiner adds that with so many organizations out there, it's not surprising that a variety of monitoring groups have arisen to keep tabs on them. One called GuideStar (www .guidestar.org) actually lets you check an organization's IRS Form 990, which groups that earn more than $25,000 a year must file with the government. By looking at a group's financials, you can see how much they earned and how that money was spent.

If that sounds tedious ("Most people don't even want to read their own tax forms," Weiner jokes), you can turn to other third-party monitoring groups like the BBB Wise Giving Alliance (www.give.org) or your local Better Business Bureau office, which keeps records on many local charities. Other watchdog groups include the American Institute of Philanthropy and Charity Navigator, both of which give groups ratings (or stars) based on mostly financial criteria.

> **There is no duty we so underrate as the duty of being happy. By being happy we sow anonymous benefits upon the world.** —*Robert Louis Stevenson*

What I have found to be the most inspiring influence on my own charitable efforts is just hearing about all the many creative ways that people find to give to the causes they believe in. It's not about how much money or time you have to give, just deciding to give anything provides the gratifying experience of connecting to what you value in the world—and connecting to others, which may be the most important aspect of giving to focus on.

The reflected glow of "doing good" is nice, but it's a shallow form of happiness. What the latest research shows is that we all gain, personally and communally, when we give to others because that giving has meaning to us, and that giving then brings us closer to our fellow humans.

Conclusion

H ere we are, at the end of a book about the many ways you can invest your money in a happier way of life. Maybe the notion of creating a happiness portfolio has you raring to go, or maybe you're wondering whether this system really works. Either way, you might be interested in hearing about my own experiences on the happiness front, and how someone who writes about money got involved in a book about quality of life.

You may know me as the personal finance columnist who started the Women in Red series for MSN Money or the writer of the "Basic Instincts" column for the *New York Times*. But before I started reporting about other people's financial issues, I was one of the countless millions who could barely cope with my own.

- I spent every dime I earned.
- My savings account was a cash-free zone.
- I got myself into a big, sticky pile of debt.
- Hedonic treadmill was my middle name.

I kept wondering when I was going to land that windfall that would save my life—and give me some more spending money. Having more money was all that mattered to me for most of my early adulthood, and in order to "have it" I used plastic to pay my way. To say that my priorities were backassward is one of the kinder descriptions you could use. Like a lot of young single women who want to live like there's no tomorrow, I had fun, I looked good. I went out almost every night. I put my vacation on Visa—because paying cash wasn't even an option. I didn't have any.

I don't know how I appeared to the rest of the world in those years, but it was a while before I looked in a mirror and faced the truth about how miserable my financial habits were making me. In fact, I don't know when I would have done so if a good friend and colleague hadn't told me about a writing job she'd heard about: MSN.com needed someone to write a down-to-earth personal finance column that would focus on real-life money issues.

Well, I had real-life money issues coming out my ears—and by now, I also had a genuine desire to resolve them. I applied for the job with the kind of zeal and conviction only a woman on the edge of her finances can muster—and got it. I have never doubted that there is a God, but this was a moment when I felt the power of a much higher wisdom in my life. Apparently I wasn't going to win the lottery, but maybe there was another way to save myself from financial chaos and collapse. Like, maybe, learning how to manage my money. I was thirty-five.

At first my columns focused on facing financial reality—and cleaning up the enormous mess of bad habits and dumb mistakes I'd made. But what I really wanted to know, and what my "cigar-chomping editor," as I liked to call him, wanted me to find out was why I had slid into such a financial swamp.

Why? What an interesting question. By now I had a couple of years of personal finance reporting under my belt, so I was well aware that my fast-mending financial problems were hardly unusual. So I began to probe beneath the common money mistakes and financial failures that people struggle with to better understand the source of the financial fantasies and delusions that were, in many cases, ruining people's lives.

As I delved into the field of behavioral economics, which explores the dynamics of people's financial behavior, things started clicking into place. I began to understand the relationship between conspicuous consumption and overspending; the mind games we play with our money; the impact of inertia, adaptation, denial, and competition on basic financial decisions—and, of course, the hedonic treadmill. The more I understood the combination of internal and external forces that influence financial behavior, the more I understood that going into debt or being unable to save or wanting more than you can possibly ever afford weren't just individual failings. They were part of a cultural malaise that directs us to do and think and act in ways that are counterproductive to our financial—and emotional—well-being.

This marked a new phase of my financial education that went

beyond making practical improvements to my own money behavior and caused me to focus more on life. This book was
partly inspired by an article about the intersection of money,
happiness, and quality of life by Cornell economist Robert
Frank, but it was also fueled by my own experience. Everything
that's in this book draws directly on what I've been through. I
didn't write these chapters because I like the research or felt
compelled to share it, but because it reflects the truth about my
own, I have to say, amazing progress.

Not that I've become a financial paragon—the Paragons met
last month and said I still didn't quite qualify—but I have mastered far more about the financial realm than I would have
dreamed was possible ten years ago. And the most powerful
lessons I've learned haven't been about my personal profit
margins, but about the profound benefits you reap when you
put less money into stuff and invest more in life.

Which leads me to the remarkable discovery I made along
this long and winding road: that by investing in happiness, not
only do you gain quality of life, you enhance your financial
well-being, too.

For example, if you hit the mall every weekend and rely on a
line of credit to regularly redecorate your home—or spice up
your wardrobe—what has that investment gotten you? The
money is gone; you have more stuff, and in some cases you have
more debt. You haven't added to your happiness or your financial health. Worse, if you then get caught up trying to keep pace
with the Joneses, or acquiring more and more material things
to sustain that buyer's high, you'll find yourself depleted emotionally and financially.

But when you shift your focus and invest more of your money in less conspicuous expenditures—enjoying life, exploring yourself, connecting to others, securing your future, and so on—the returns are so much greater. You've enriched your all-around quality of life so that inner craving for stuff abates. You may spend as much as you once did at the mall, but the satisfaction you receive is deeper. And because you're channeling your money into living, not buying—which includes easing financial stress and saving for the future—your fiscal picture improves. Here, a humble diagram to show you what I mean.

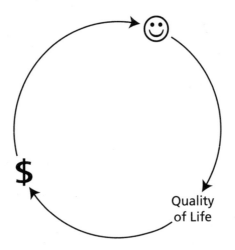

In other words, the laws of happiness favor the financial investor. Or maybe the laws of finance favor the happiness investor. All I know is that if you are seeking financial sanity, put your money where your happiness lies. You will find yourself spending less on things that don't matter—and more on the aspects of life that tend to hold their value—which will both increase your overall joy in life and keep you fiscally on track.

It's a simple system. Try it sometime. After all, it is your life, and it's up to you to make it a happy one.

ACKNOWLEDGMENTS

I've given up all hope of being able to express in one short section the gratitude I feel toward so many people.

First let me say to those who know me, professionally or personally or both, you may not see your name here, but this is my thank-you to you, for being there, for listening, for what you said and what you didn't say, the e-mail you sent, that phone call you made, the hug you might have thought was just a hug—but to me it wasn't—thank you for a thousand kind, smart, unforgettable things. I can't do justice to them all here, but I want you to know that I remember.

A special thanks to Eden Ross Lipson, who has been both a blessing and a role model in my life. A huge thanks to my incomparable agent, Neeti Madan, who has made me a contented little writer, indeed. An equally big thanks to my talented editor, Becky Cole, for bringing me to this project and for the excellent guidance she gave this first-time author.

In the "This book would not exist without . . ." category, I owe Richard Jenkins such immense thanks, all I can hope is that this book sells enough copies so I can buy him that yacht he wants.

I'm not sure where I'd be without Paula Derrow and Caroline Hwang—who talked me down from the trees more times than I can count. I'd also like to thank Greg Lichtenberg for the most amazing writing class ever, in which I met Lisa Montanarelli and Amy Benson, who did more than they know to keep me on track. My deepest respect and appreciation to Jeff Sommer for hiring me, editing me, and helping "Basic Instincts" to grow— and to Mickey Meece for her sharp feedback and warm words.

Gotta thank the girls: first, the Women in Red—Anna, Beth, Brice, Carole, Lyndsey, Stephanie, Tricia—y'all rock. Then my nearest and dearest, in no particular order: Val, Kathleen, Athina, Melanie, Alicia, and Yalitza. And Kurt for being Kurt.

Last, a big thank-you to all those who generously shared their time, their thoughts, and sometimes their family and friends for this book: Hazen, Susan, Wendy, Peter, Elaine, Steve, Beth Clarke, Kate Hanley, Brice Gaillard, Monnie, Elizabeth, Vincent, Carmi, Sylvia, Rachel, Mark, Jacqueline Blix, Glen Firebaugh, Richard Easterlin, Andrew Oswald, Amanda Goodall, Mihalyi Csikszentmihalyi, John Helliwell, and Bill Schultheis.

I wish I could do more than just thank my parents. Now that

I am a parent myself, my appreciation for all they did and continue to do cannot be put into words. That goes double, at least, for my husband, who kept my spirits up and my butt glued to my chair when I was finishing this project—and who makes me happier than anything or anyone, except possibly Connor.

BIBLIOGRAPHY

Bargh, John A., Tanya L. Chartrand, 1999. The Unbearable Automaticity of Being, *American Psychologist*, 54, 462–479.

Bender, Keith A., Natalia A. Jivan, 2005. What Makes Retirees Happy?, Center for Retirement Research, Issue in Brief, 28 (February).

Blix, Jacqueline, David Heitmiller, 1997. *Getting a Life*, Penguin.

Brown, Stephanie L., R. Michael Brown, 2006. Selective Investment Theory: Recasting the Functional Significance of Close Relationships, *Psychological Inquiry*, 17(1), 1–29.

Clark, Andrew E., Andrew J. Oswald, 1996. Satisfaction and Comparison Income, *Journal of Public Economics*, 61, 359–381.

Csikszentmihalyi, Mihaly, 2003. Materialism and the Evolution of Consciousness. In *Psychology and Consumer Culture: The Struggle for a*

Good Life in a Materialistic World, Tim Kasser, Allen D. Kanner (eds.), American Psychological Association.

Easterlin, Richard A., 2001. Income and Happiness: Towards a Unified Theory, *The Economic Journal*, 111 (July), 465–484.

———, 2005. A Puzzle for Adaptive Theory, *Journal of Economic Behavior & Organization*, 56 (4), 513–521.

Frank, Robert H., 2004. How Not to Buy Happiness, *Daedalus*, 133 (2), 69–79.

———, 1999. *Luxury Fever*, The Free Press.

Frank, Robert H., Adam Seth Levine, 2005. Expenditure Cascades, Cornell University mimeograph.

Helliwell, John F., 2003. How's Life? Combining Individual and National Variables to Explain Subjective Well-Being, *Economic Modeling*, 20 (March), 331–360.

Honoré, Carl, 2004. *In Praise of Slowness*, HarperSanFrancisco.

Layard, Richard, 2003. Happiness: Has Social Science Got a Clue?, Lectures 1–3; Lionel Robbins Memorial Lectures, London School of Economics.

———, 2005. *Happiness: Lessons From a New Science*, Penguin.

Lykken, David, Auke Tellegen, 1996. Happiness Is a Stochastic Phenomenon, *Psychological Science*, 7 (3).

Lyubomirsky, Sonja, Kennon M. Sheldon, David Schkade, 2005. Pursuing Happiness: The Architecture of Sustainable Change, *Review of General Psychology*, 9 (2), 111–131.

Miller, Jody, Matt Miller. Get A Life!, *Fortune*, November 2005.

Nettle, Daniel, 2005. *Happiness: The Science Behind Your Smile*, Oxford.

Neumark, David, Andrew Postlewaite, 1998. Relative Income Concerns and the Rise in Married Women's Employment, *Journal of Public Economics*, 70, 157–183.

O'Neill, Barbara, Benoit Sorhaindo, Jing Jian Xiao, E. Thomas Garman, 2005. Negative Health Effects of Financial Stress, *Consumer Interests Annual*, 51.

Oswald, Andrew, David Blanchflower, 2004. Money, Sex, and Happiness: An Empirical Study, *Scandinavian Journal of Economics*, 106, 393–416.

Oswald, Andrew, Liam Graham, 2006. Hedonic Capital, working paper.

Rojas, Mariano, The Complexity of Well-Being: A Life Satisfaction Conception and a Domains-of-Life Approach. In *Researching Well-Being in Developing Countries*, I. Gough, A. J. McGregor (eds.), Cambridge University Press, 2006.

Schwartz, Barry. The Tyranny of Choice, *Scientific American*, April 2004.

Seligman, Martin E. P., 2002. *Authentic Happiness*, The Free Press.

Solnick, Sara J., David Hemenway, 1998. Is More Always Better?: A Survey on Positional Concerns, *Journal of Economic Behavior & Organization*, 37, 373–383.

Sull, Donald N., Dominic Houlder, 2005. Do Your Commitments Match Your Convictions?, *Harvard Business Review*, January.

Thaler, Richard H., Shlomo Benartzi, 2004. Save More Tomorrow: Using Behavioral Economics to Increase Employee Saving, *Journal of Political Economy*, 112 (1), S164–S187.

Zimmerman, Anke, 2005. Chasing the Good Life: Life Cycle Aspirations for Goods, Family, Work, and Health, University of Southern California, unpublished manuscript.

INDEX

Index

Index

ABOUT THE AUTHOR

MP Dunleavey writes the award-winning "Women in Red" series for the MSN Money Web site and the "Basic Instincts" column for the *New York Times*. She lives in upstate New York with her husband and son. This is her first book, and she's pretty happy about that.

8/07